REDEMPTION
TRUTHS

BOOKS BY SIR ROBERT ANDERSON

REDEMPTION TRUTHS

SIR ROBERT ANDERSON

Foreword by
Arnold Fair

Biographical Sketch by
Warren W. Wiersbe

KREGEL PUBLICATIONS
Grand Rapids, Michigan 49501

Redemption Truths, by Sir Robert Anderson. © 1980 by
Kregel Publications, a division of Kregel, Inc. P. O. Box
2607, Grand Rapids, MI 49501. All rights reserved.

Cover Design: Art Jacobs

Library of Congress Cataloging-in-Publication Data

Anderson, Robert, Sir, 1841-1918.
    Redemption Truths.

    (Sir Robert Anderson library)
    Reprint of the ed. published by Gospel Publishing
House, New York under title: "For Us Men."
    1. Salvation. I. Title.
III. Series. Anderson, Robert, Sir. 1841-1918

BT751.A58   1980   234   80-16161
                                                              CIP
ISBN   0-8254-2131-4 (pbk.)

7 8 9 / 03 02 01 00 99

Printed in the United States of America

CONTENTS

FOREWORD

Like the pure prestine beauty of an unsoiled lily as it unfolds in the fruition and fragrance of God's creative purpose, so Sir Robert Anderson presents *Redemption Truths*. The gift offer of salvation is simply presented. The glory of sonship is challengingly offered. The grandeur of eternity's splendor is shown.

Redemption Truths is a wonderful book to present to a new Christian. Here are many scriptural answers to the myriad of questions that flood a new believer's mind. However, the author does not merely answer questions, he stimulates the inquiring person to further study. He presents unique insights that only the Holy Spirit of God could give to a keen, clean perceptive mind. This makes this book a valuable tool for the pastor, evangelist, and student of God's Word.

Sir Robert Anderson was a legally powerful man of the 19th century. He was head of the criminal investigation department of Scotland Yard and the political crime advisor to the British Home Office. Not only was he in a God-given place of power, but he associated with and had an appreciation of authority. Could this be the reason that, in so much of Sir Robert Anderson's writing, he takes the position of an apologist? He is uniquely a defender of the truth. He believed and wrote that God's Word is absolute truth to be trusted and lived. As an investigator of crime, he wanted only factual reality not fiction. He found this truth in the Lord Jesus Christ, and the fervency of his desire, to share this truth with others, burns through these pages.

One is captivated by scriptural principles presented with depth and practicality. As you mount his staircase of truths you will find them etched with personal experiences of inspiration and insights. He draws from history in Chapter 9 and others to teach truths that should be obvious.

The reader will receive much that will redeem his mind and thoughts from the futility of this earthly scene. The panorama of the truths of redemption will live in new meaningfulness. May redemption truths be received and lived by each reader.

J. ARNOLD FAIR

BIOGRAPHICAL SKETCH

Sir Robert Anderson described himself as "an anglicized Irishman of Scottish extraction." Before his death in 1918, he was widely recognized as a popular lay-preacher, an author of best-selling books on Biblical subjects, and one of the most capable "defenders of the faith" at a time when the "higher criticism" was threatening the church.

Robert Anderson was born in 1841 in Dublin, where his father, Matthew Anderson, served as Crown Solicitor for the city. His father was also a distinguished elder in the Irish Presbyterian Church. Robert was educated privately in Dublin, Paris, and Boulogne; and in 1859 he entered Trinity College, Dublin, graduating in 1862.

Brought up in a devout Christian home, Anderson in his late teens had serious doubts about his own conversion. About that time (1859-60) the Irish Revival was touching and changing the lives of many, including Robert's sister. She persuaded her brother to attend one of the services, but the popular hymns disturbed him and he got very little out of the message. The following Sunday, he attended church and heard Dr. John Hall preach at the evening service. The message so disturbed him that he remained to argue with the preacher.

In telling of the experience, Anderson wrote: "...facing me as we stood upon the pavement, he repeated with great solemnity his message and appeal: 'I tell you as a minister of Christ and in His name that there is life for you here and now, if you will accept Him. Will you accept Christ or will you reject Him?' After a pause — how prolonged I know not — I exclaimed, 'In God's name I will accept Christ.' ...And I turned homeward with the peace of God filling my heart."

Two years later, Anderson was active as a lay-preacher and was greatly used to win many to Christ. In 1863 he was made a member of the Irish Bar and served on the legal circuit. About this time, the Fenians were at work (a secret society attempting to overthrow British rule in Ireland), and he became involved interrogating prisoners and preparing legal briefs. This was his introduction into police work.

He was married in 1873 and four years later moved to London as a member of the Home Office staff. He had access to the detective department and made good use of it. In 1888, while Jack the Ripper was terrorizing London, Anderson moved into Scotland Yard as Assistant Commissioner of Metropolitan Police and Chief of the Criminal Investigation Department. He served his country well until his retirement in 1901, and the records show that crime decreased in London during that period. Conan Doyle was entertaining London at that time with his Sherlock Holmes stories, but it was

Anderson and his staff who were ridding the city of crime and criminals.

Anderson had a large circle of friends, not only politicians but especially preachers: Dr. Handley G. Moule, J. Stuart Holden, Henry Drummond, James M. Gray, Ç.I. Scofield, A.C. Dixon, and E.W. Bullinger, whose views on Israel and the church greatly influenced Anderson. It was Horatius Bonar who first taught Anderson the great truths concerning the second coming of Christ, and "the blessed hope" was a precious doctrine to him, especially during the dark days of the first war.

He authored seventeen major books on Biblical themes, and it is good to see them coming back into print. Charles H. Spurgeon said that Anderson's book *Human Destiny* was "the most valuable contribution on the subject" that he had ever seen. His last book, *Unfulfilled Prophecy and the Hope of the Church*, was published in 1917. These books underscore the inspiration and dependable authority of the Bible, the deity of Jesus Christ, and the necessity of new birth. He tracked down myths and religious error, arrested and exposed it, with the same skill and courage that he displayed when he tracked down criminals. If you have never met Sir Robert Anderson, then you are about to embark on a thrilling voyage of discovery. If he is already one of your friends, then finding a new Anderson title, or meeting an old one, will bring joy to your heart and enlightenment to your mind. Happy reading!

WARREN W. WIERSBE

How A Sinner Can Be Saved

"A certain Samaritan, as he journeyed, came where he was; and when he saw him, he had compassion on him."

Luke 10:33.

1

HOW A SINNER CAN BE SAVED

"WHAT shall I do to inherit eternal life?" The question was framed by a professional theologian, to test the orthodoxy of the great Rabbi of Nazareth. For evidently it was rumoured that the new Teacher was telling the people of a short road to Heaven.

And the answer given was clear—no other answer, indeed, is possible; for what a man *inherits* is his by right—eternal life is the reward and goal of a perfect life on earth. A *perfect* life, mark—the standard being perfect love to God and man.

And this being so, no one but a Pharisee or a fool could dream of *inheriting* eternal life; and the practical question which concerns every one of us is whether God has provided a way by which men who are not perfect, but sinful, can be saved. And the answer to this question is hidden in the parable by which the Lord silenced his interrogator's quibble, " Who is my neighbour ? "

Here is the story.[1] A traveller on the downward road to the city of the Curse fell among thieves, who robbed and wounded him, and flung him down, half dead, by the wayside. First, a priest came that way, and then a Levite, who looked at him, and passed on. Why a priest and a Levite ? Did the Lord intend to throw contempt upon religion and the law ? That is quite incredible. No ; but He wished to teach what, even after nineteen centuries of Christianity, not one person in a thousand seems to know, that law and religion can do nothing for a ruined and dead sinner. A sinner needs *a Saviour*. And so the Lord brings the Samaritan upon the scene.

But why *a Samaritan* ? Just because " Jews have no dealings with Samaritans." Save as a last resource, no Jew would accept deliverance from such a quarter. Sin not only spells danger and death to the sinner, but it alienates the heart from God. Nothing but a sense of utter helplessness and hopelessness will lead him to

---

[1] Luke x. 30–35.

throw himself, with abject self-renunciation, at the feet of Christ.

Not that man by nature is necessarily vicious or immoral. It is chiefly in the spiritual sphere that the effects of the Eden Fall declare themselves. Under human teaching the Fall becomes an adequate excuse for a sinful life. But the Word of God declares that men are "without excuse." For although "they that are in the flesh cannot please God," they can lead clean and honest and honourable lives. The "cannot" is not in the moral, but in the spiritual, sphere. For "the mind of the flesh is enmity against God; for it is not subject to the law of God."[1]

And this affords a clue to the essential character of sin. In the lowest classes of the community sin is but another word for crime. At a higher level in the social scale it is regarded as equivalent to vice. And in a still higher sphere the element of impiety is taken into account. But all this is arbitrary and false. Crime and vice and impiety are unquestionably sinful; but yet the most upright and moral and religious of men may be the greatest sinner upon earth.

[1] Romans viii. 7, 8, R.V.

Why state this hypothetically? It is *a fact*; witness the life and character of Saul of Tarsus. Were the record not accredited by Paul the inspired Apostle, we might well refuse to believe that such blamelessness and piety and zeal were ever attained by mortal man.[1] Why then does the Apostle call himself the chief of sinners? Was this an outburst of wild exaggeration, of the kind to which pious folk of an hysterical turn are addicted? It was the sober acknowledgment of the well-known principle that privilege increases responsibility and deepens guilt.

According to the "humanity gospel," which is to-day supplanting the Gospel of Christ in so many pulpits, the man was a pattern saint. In the judgment of God he was a pattern sinner. And just because he had, as judged by men, attained pre-eminence in saintship, Divine grace taught him to own his pre-eminence in sin. With all his zeal for God, and fancied godliness, he

---

[1] In presence of those to whom he was well known, he could say, "I have lived before God in all good conscience until this day" (Acts xxiii. 1, R.V.). And with reference to his past life, he could write, "As touching the righteousness which is in the law, found blameless" (Philippians iii. 6, R.V.).

awoke to find that he was a blasphemer. And what a blasphemer! Who would care a straw what a Jerusalem mob thought of the Rabbi of Nazareth? But who would not be influenced by the opinion of Gamaliel's great disciple?

An infidel has said that "Thou shalt not steal" is merely the language of the hog in the clover, to warn off the hogs outside the fence. And this reproach attaches to all mere human conceptions of sin. Men judge of sin by its results; and their estimate of its results is coloured by their own interests. But all such conceptions of sin are inadequate. Definitions are rare in Scripture, but sin is there defined for us. It may show itself in transgression, or in failing to come up to a standard. But essentially it is lawlessness; which means, not transgression of law, nor absence of law, but revolt against law—in a word, self-will. This is the very essence of sin. The perfect life was the life of Him who never did His own will, but only and always the will of God. All that is short of this, or different from this, is characterised as sin.

And here it is not a question of acts merely, but of the mind and heart. Man's whole nature is at fault. Even human law recognises this principle. In the case of ordinary crime we take the rough and ready method of dealing with men for what they do. But not so in crime of the highest kind. Treason consists in the hidden thought of the heart. Overt acts of disloyalty or violence are not the crime, but merely the evidence of the crime. The crime is the purpose of which such acts give proof. Men cannot read the heart; they can judge of the purpose only by words and acts. But it is not so with God. In His sight the treason of the human heart is manifest, and no outward acts are needed to declare it.

The truest test of a man is not conduct, but character; not what he does, but what he is. Human judgment must, of course, be guided by a man's acts and words. But God is not thus limited. Man judges character by conduct; God judges conduct by character. Therefore it is that " what is highly esteemed among men is abomination in the sight of God."

And this brings us back to the case of Paul. Under the influence of environment, and following his natural bent, he took to religion as another man might take to vice. Religion was his speciality. And the result was a splendid success. Here was the case of a man who really "did his best," and whose "best" was a "record" achievement. But what was God's judgment of it all? What was his own, when he came to look back on it from the Cross of Christ? Surveying the innumerable hosts of the sinners of mankind, he says, "*of whom I am chief.*" And this, as already urged, because his unrivalled "proficiency" in religion had raised him to the very highest pinnacle of privilege and responsibility, and thus proved him to be the wickedest and worst of men.

"But I obtained mercy," he adds. Not because he had sinned "ignorantly in unbelief"; for that plea counts for nothing here, though it led the Lord to extend further mercy to him on his repentance. He was twice mercied: first in receiving salvation, and next in being called to the Apostleship; for it is not God's way to put blasphemers into the ministry. But the mercy of his salvation was only and altogether because "Christ Jesus came into the world to save sinners." [1] He had no other plea.

---

[1] 1 Timothy i. 15.

The Apostle Paul's case only illustrates the principle of Divine judgment, as proclaimed by the Lord Himself in language of awful solemnity. The most terrible doom recorded in Old Testament history was that which engulfed the Cities of the Plain. And yet the Lord declared that a still direr doom awaited the cities which had been specially favoured by His presence and ministry on earth. The sin of Sodom we know. But what had Capernaum done? Religion flourished there. It was "exalted to Heaven" by privilege, and there is no suggestion that evil practices prevailed. The exponents of the "humanity gospel," now in popular favour, would have deemed it a model community. They would tell us, moreover, that if Sodom was really destroyed by a storm of fire and brimstone, it was Jewish ignorance which attributed the catastrophe to their cruel Jehovah God. The kind, good "Jesus" of *their* enlightened theology would have far different thoughts about Capernaum!

" But I say unto you," was the Lord's last warning to that seemingly happy and peaceful community, "it shall be more tolerable for the land of Sodom in the Day of Judgment, than for thee." [1]

What, then, we may well ask, had Capernaum done? So far, as the record tells us, absolutely nothing. Had there been flagrant immorality, or active hostility, the Lord would not have made His home there; nor would it have come to be called "His own city." [2] And had there been aggressive unbelief, the "mighty works" which He wrought so lavishly among its people would have been restrained. Thoroughly respectable and religious folk they evidently were. But "they repented not"; that was all.

That such people should be deemed guiltier than Sodom, and that the champion religionist of His own age should rank as the greatest sinner of any age: here is an enigma that is insoluble if we ignore the Eden Fall—that "degrading dogma," as it is now called, of the corruption of our nature—and the teaching of Scripture as to the essential character of sin. It was not that these men, knowing God, rejected Him, but that they did not know Him. "He was in the world, and

---

[1] Matthew xi. 24.   [2] Matthew iv. 13; ix. 1; *cf.* Mark ii. 1.

the world was made by Him, and the world knew Him not."

" But," the record adds, " as many as received Him, to them gave He the right to become children of God." On receiving Him, or, in other words, on believing on His name, they were " born of God." [1]

If sin were merely a matter of wrong-doing, if it was not " in the blood," if our very nature was not spiritually corrupt and depraved by it—a new birth would be unnecessary. A blind man does not see things in a wrong light; he cannot see them at all. And man by nature is spiritually blind. He " cannot *see* the Kingdom of God," much less enter it. He *must* be born again.

But there is more in sin than this. It not only depraves the sinner, but it brings him under judgment. Guilt attaches to it. Salvation, therefore, must be through redemption, and redemption can only be by blood.

---

[1] John i. 10–13, R.V.

Significance of the Passover

"The kindness and love of God our Saviour toward man."

Titus 3:4.

2

SIGNIFICANCE OF THE PASSOVER

THE Bible is the story of redemption. Its opening chapters are a preface which tells how God made man in His own image; how man fell by sin; how iniquity abounded until there was no remedy; how the judgment of the Flood prepared the way for a new departure; how man again apostatized; and how God then took up a favoured people, a "first-born," to serve as His agent and witness upon earth. The rest of the Old Testament is the history, not of the human race, but of "Abraham and his seed." Its deeper spiritual teaching relates to the true "Seed," the true "First-born," the Lord Jesus Christ.

Genesis closes by telling how the favoured people came to be sojourners in Egypt. As we open the Book of Exodus we find that, from being the honoured guests of Pharaoh, they had become slaves, oppressed by hard and cruel bondage.

Their struggles for freedom only served to rivet their fetters. To work out their destiny was impossible until they had been delivered from Egyptian slavery; and deliverance was impossible save by the power of God. But before they could be redeemed by power, they must needs be redeemed by blood.

The key-picture of our redemption story is perfect even in details. Being in Egypt, they came under Egypt's doom; for in the types the first-born represented the family, and the Divine decree was that "all the first-born in the land of Egypt shall die." There was no exemption for Israel.

But a "way of salvation" was proclaimed. The paschal lamb was to be killed for every house, and its blood sprinkled upon the door. Here was the Gospel message which Moses brought from their Jehovah God: "When He seeth the blood upon the lintel and on the two side posts, the Lord will pass over the door, and will not suffer the destroyer to come into your houses to smite you." [1]

The blood of "slain beasts" could never take

---
[1] Exodus xii. 23.

away sin, or change a sinner's condition or destiny. But it could foreshadow the death of Christ, the great Passover of our redemption. And the meaning of " blood " is death *applied*. Therefore it is that, in the Divine accuracy which marks the language of Scripture, redemption is by " blood." It is only for those who by faith become one with Christ in His death.

We learn from the typology of Exodus, and from the express teaching of the New Testament, that the Passover was but the first step in the full redemption of the people. But it was the foundation of all the rest, and therefore it is well to pause here, and to mark its significance.

But why, it may be asked, should we study Exodus, when the New Testament lies open before us? The ready answer is, that never in the history of Christendom was the typology of the Pentateuch more needed than to-day. So utter is the blindness, so deep the apostasy, of the present hour, that on every hand popular leaders of religious thought are commending, as the outcome of a new enlightenment, a Gospel that betrays ignorance of " the first principles of the oracles of God "—the very A B C of the Divine revelation to mankind.

In this theology sin is but a defect, inevitable in the progress of the race toward the perfection which is man's natural destiny. The underside of the tapestry, of course, looks blurred and foul. And "evil is only the underside of good." [1] But all will come right in the end. The doctrines of original sin and vicarious sacrifice belong to the childhood of the race, and in these days of ours it is time to break with the nursery.

We may well exclaim, in the words of Bonar's "Hymn for the Last Days" :—

> " Evil is now our good,
>   And error is our truth ! "

Written half a century ago, these words were almost prophetic. No less so are words that follow :—

> " The cross is growing old,
>   And the great Sepulchre
>   Is but a Hebrew tomb ;
>   The Christ has died in vain."

---

[1] These are the words of one of the most popular exponents of the new Gospel. I quote them without pretending to understand them.

" The Christ of ages past
  Is now the Christ no more ;
  Altar and fire are gone,
  The Victim but a dream."

We have come to such a pass that the most elementary truths of Scripture need to be restated—man's utter ruin and hopelessness, consequent upon the spiritual depravity that is his heritage from the Fall ; and his need of "redemption by blood "—salvation through the death of Christ.

And we need not only to have Scriptural truth, but to have truth Scripturally expressed. The present-day revolt against orthodox doctrines is due in part to the manner in which those doctrines have been formulated. One great school of theology has taken its stand upon the sin-offering ; and, ignoring the redemption sacrifices, it unduly limits the scope and efficacy of the work of Christ. Another school bases its Gospel on the teaching of the Passover, and ignores all that follows. As already indicated, the sin-offering, in its various aspects, was only for a redeemed people ;

---

[1] But the stranger could ally himself with the Covenant people, and obtain the blessings of the Covenant. Let us not be misled by the critics into supposing that the Divine Mosaic code was harsh to the stranger. There never was a code more considerate or kind. (See, *ex. gr.*, Leviticus xxv. 35 ; Numbers xv. 15–29 ; Deuteronomy x. 18, 19 ; xiv. 29 ; xvi. 11 ; xxiii. 7 ; xxiv. 17–21 ; xxvi. 11–13.)

and it was by the Passover that they obtained redemption. And further, as we shall find in the sequel, the full revelation of grace in the New Testament transcends all that the types can teach us.

But let us begin at the beginning, and trace the successive steps indicated in the key-pictures of the Pentateuch. No one must suppose, of course, that the blessings prefigured by the types come to the believer in a chronological sequence, or that they are separated by intervals of time. But in the key-pictures these stages are clearly distinguished, in order that our minds may dwell upon them, and that thus we may learn in all its fulness what the redemption of Christ has won for us.

We all know the story, do we not? Well, we think we do—how God passed through the land in judgment, and how when He came to the blood-sprinkled door He passed it over, instead of entering in to slay the first-born. But what if we should find that this is not at all what the record teaches?

In dealing with a dead language, etymology may sometimes afford a clue to the meaning of a word, but the only safe and certain guide to its meaning is its use.

This verb, *pasach*, which occurs three times in Exodus xii. (verses 13, 23, and 27), is used in three other passages of Scripture, namely, 2 Samuel iv. 4 ; 1 Kings xviii. 21 and 26 ; and Isaiah xxxi. 5. A careful study of these passages will confirm a first impression that the meaning usually given to the word is really foreign to it.

In 2 Samuel iv. 4 it is translated, " became lame," a rendering which its use in 1 Kings xviii. 26 may serve to explain. We there read that the prophets of Baal *leaped* about their altar. Their action was not, as has been grotesquely suggested, " a religious dance " ; it betokened the physical paroxysms of demon-possessed men. Having worked themselves into a state of religious frenzy, they leaped up and down, round the altar.

The meaning of the word in the twenty-first verse may seem wholly apart from both these uses ; but it is not so. " How long *halt* ye between two opinions ? " The word " halt " is here used, not in the sense of stopping dead, like a soldier at the word of command, but of hesitating to take the decisive step to the one side or the other. If the verb *pasach* meant to "pass over," it would express precisely what the prophet called upon the people to do, and what they ought to have done, but would not do. But a careful study of its use in the passages cited—going lame, halting, leaping—will show that the essential thought is the *kind of action* implied in each case, and that the thought of passing away is foreign to it. The action of a bird in fluttering over its nest would exactly illustrate it.

And now, with the help of the clue thus gained, the last of these passages will shed a flood of new light upon the Exodus story. "As birds flying, so will the Lord of Hosts protect Jerusalem ; He will protect and deliver it. He will *pass over* and preserve it." [1] How does a mother bird—the word is in the feminine—protect her nest ? Is it by passing over it in the sense of passing it by ? Deuteronomy xxxii. 11 describes the eagle "fluttering over her young." Though the word here used is different, the thought is identical. As a bird protects her nest, so does God preserve His people. He "rideth upon the heavens for their help"; He hides them under

---

[1] Isaiah xxxi. 5 (R.V.).

the shadow of His wings, "the wings of the Al-
mighty." [1]   And thus it was that He preserved
them on that awful night when the destroyer
was abroad in the land of Egypt.

What is done by God's command, He is said to
do Himself. Hence the language of verse 23 :
"The Lord will pass through to smite the Egyp-
tians." But the words that follow make it clear
that it was not the Lord Himself who executed
the judgment—words indeed could not be clearer :
" And when He seeth the blood upon the lintel
and on the two side posts, *the Lord* will pass
over the door, and *will not suffer the destroyer
to come in unto your houses to smite you.*" The
highest thought suggested by the conventional
reading of the passage, is that He spared them ;
the truth is that He stood on guard, as it were,
at every blood-sprinkled door. He became their
Saviour. Nothing short of this is the meaning
of the Passover.

The faith of His people in the old time might
well put to shame the half-faith of so many of
His people in these days of the fuller light of

---

[1] Psalm xvii. 8 ; *cf.* Psalm xxxvi. 7 ; lvii. 1 ; lxi. 4 ; lxiii. 7 ;
xci. 4.

the Christian revelation. *They* learned to sing, " Behold, *God is my salvation* ; I will trust, and not be afraid ; for the Lord Jehovah is my strength and my song ; *He also is become my salvation.*"[1]

The Divine religion of Judaism was marked by festivals based on sacrifice—joy in the presence of God, based on atonement for sin. And so is it in Christianity. Hence the exhortation, " For our Passover also hath been sacrificed, even Christ: wherefore let us keep festival!"[2] And this should be realized in every Christian life. Festival-keeping speaks of joy, and joy is the very atmosphere of Christianity. Not the gaiety of fools, which any passing sorrow kills ; but joy so firmly based on eternal realities, that passing storms of sorrow, let them be never so fierce, cannot quench it. "Sorrowful, yet always rejoicing" is one of the paradoxes of the Christian life.

---

[1] Exodus xv. 2 ; Isaiah xii. 2.
[2] 1 Corinthians v. 7, 8 (R.V., *marg.*).

Fulness of Our Redemption

"Christ being come an high priest of good things to come, . . .entered in once for all into the holy place, having obtained eternal redemption for us."
Hebrews 9:11,12.

3

FULNESS OF OUR REDEMPTION

THE story of the Passover teaches the great truth that salvation is God's work altogether, and that a sinner can be saved only through redemption. And it teaches the further truth that he must be saved as he is and where he is, in his ruin and helplessness and guilt. If a sinner could not be saved *in his sins*, salvation would be impossible, for there is no power of recovery in him. But this is only the beginning. God alone can take him out of the horrible pit and out of the miry clay. But God does do this, and He sets his feet upon a rock, and establishes his goings, and puts a new song in his mouth.

Israel was delivered from Egypt and its bondage as well as from its doom. Redemption by blood, was followed by redemption by power. With a strong hand were they brought out, and their deliverance was not complete until they stood upon the wilderness-side of the sea, and saw their enemies dead upon the shore—saw the power that had enslaved them broken. "*Then* sang Moses and the children of Israel this song unto the Lord, I will sing unto the Lord, for He hath triumphed gloriously: the horse and his rider hath He thrown into the sea. The Lord is my strength and song, and He is become my salvation."[1]

But even this does not exhaust the fulness of redemption. The words of 1 Corinthians i. 30 may serve as a heading for what is to follow, but a defect in our English translations of the passage obscures its meaning. If man were merely blind and foolish and ignorant, Divine wisdom would meet all his need. But as a sinner he stands guilty and condemned; and, more than this, sin has corrupted and defiled him: and without holiness there can be no fellowship with God. Therefore it is that, in the fulness of our salvation, Christ is made unto us not only wisdom from God, but also redemption—complete redemption, including *both* righteousness and sanctification.[2] He

---

[1] Exodus xv. 1, 2.

[2] Both A.V. and R.V. ignore the word *both* in the passage, and the *both* requires the last *and* to be rendered "even," for redemption is a blessing not additional to, but inclusive of, righteousness and sanctification. The construction is the same as in ver. 24 (both Jews and Greeks).

is made unto us everything which our condition needs. He not merely saves us from death, He brings us to God.

The release of a person who stands charged with an offence, gives him neither right nor fitness to approach his Sovereign, much less to live in the palace; and no such gulf separates a king from his meanest subject as that which yawns between a sinner and a thrice-holy God. Forgiveness of sins could give neither title nor fitness to draw near to the Divine Majesty. It might ensure exemption from hell, but it certainly could give no right to heaven. But redemption is more than mere forgiveness. Christ satisfies the sinner's need in all its variety and depth.

But, someone may demand, why should we notice these distinctions? Just because we are apt entirely to misjudge both the need and the grace that meets it, and to regard as mere matters of course the heaped-up gifts which grace has lavished on us. In this sphere nothing is a matter of course. Every added blessing should increase our wonder and deepen our worship, at the boundlessness of Divine grace, and the perfectness of the redemption that is ours in Christ.

The twelfth chapter of Exodus tells of deliverance from the doom of Egypt; and the immediate sequel tells of triumphant deliverance from the power of Egypt. This goes far beyond the conventional appreciation of the Gospel in these days of ours; and yet we learn from the nineteenth chapter that God's attitude toward the people thus favoured and blest was one of stern exclusion and repulsion. Warning after warning was given them not to come near to Him. They must not touch even the base of the mountain on which He was about to manifest His presence. His command to Moses was, "Go down, charge the people, lest they break through unto the Lord to gaze, and many of them perish."[1] Moses, who typified "the Mediator of the New Covenant," might approach; but as for the people, they were warned off at the peril of their lives.

And in the twenty-fourth chapter, after the law had been given, the prohibition was repeated. "Worship ye afar off," was the Divine command even to Aaron and the elders. " Moses alone shall come near the Lord; but they shall not come

---

[1] Exodus xix. 12, 13, 21, 24.

nigh, neither shall the people go up with him."
But now mark the amazing change that resulted
from the events recorded in that chapter. "All
the words of the Lord, and all the judgments"
were recorded in a book. An altar was set up;
and burnt-offerings were offered, and peace-offer-
ings sacrificed. The blood of the covenant was
sprinkled upon the book and upon the people—
here, no doubt, as on other occasions, the elders
standing for the whole congregation. And mark
the sequel. "*Then* went up Moses, and Aaron,
Nadab, and Abihu, and seventy of the elders of
Israel; and they saw the God of Israel, . . .
and upon the nobles of the children of Israel He
laid not His hand: also they saw God, and did eat
and drink." [1]

But yesterday it would have been death to them
to look on God; now "they saw God," and so perfectly were they at rest in His presence that they
"did eat and drink." The sceptic will ask, with
a sneer, How could "the blood of calves and
goats" produce a change so wonderful? But he
will not sneer if you tell him that the transfer
of a few bits of crumpled paper could change

---

[1] Exodus xxiv. 8-11.

the condition of the recipient from pauperism to wealth.

The bank-note paper in itself is absolutely worthless; but it represents gold in the coffers of the Bank of England. In itself "the blood of slain beasts" was of no value whatsoever; but it represented "the precious blood of Christ," of infinitely greater worth than gold. In one day a pauper may be thus raised from penury to affluence. In one day Israel was thus established as a holy people in covenant with God. For it is by "the blood of the covenant" that the sinner is sanctified—the same blood by which the covenant is dedicated.[1]

And what is the next scene in the great Pentateuchal drama of redemption? To the very people, who had stood in terror, beyond the bounds which shut them out from Sinai, the command is given, "Let them make Me a sanctuary; that I may dwell among them."[2] The distance is infinite which separates even the best of men from God. But in Christ, and in virtue of His finished work, even the worst of men from being "far off" may be "made nigh."[3]

---

[1] Hebrews x. 29.   [2] Exodus xxv. 8.   [3] Ephesians ii. 13, 14.

And these blessings, and the place of privilege pertaining to them, create new needs and new responsibilities. For a sinner unredeemed, and alienated from God there can be no possible need of a place of worship; but a place of worship is a necessity for one who has " obtained access," and who is called to fellowship with God. And if a place of worship, there must also be a priest. The next step, therefore, in this great " passion play " is the call of Aaron to the priesthood. Chapter xxiv. records the sanctification of the people; the next three chapters relate to the place of worship; and chapter xxviii. to the appointment of the priest.

One of the vital errors of apostate Christianity is the false position it assigns to the priestly office. A priest had no part in procuring redemption for Israel. The Passover was not a priestly sacrifice. By the head of the house it was that the lamb was killed, and its blood sprinkled on the door. And it was the head of the house who presided at the supper. In none of the paschal rites, from first to last, was there either need or room for priestly action. And the great burnt-offerings of the covenant were not priestly sacrifices. The occasional mention of priests in the earlier chapters of Exodus has suggested to some that, prior to the appointment of Aaron, the heads of houses had priestly powers. But such a suggestion is vetoed here. The language used is strikingly significant. " *Young men of the children of Israel* " were the offerers.[1] The inference is plain that those who killed the victims had no official position whatsoever. Moses it was, not Aaron, who sprinkled the blood; and Moses was not a priest, he was the *mediator* of the covenant.

Both the possibility and the need of establishing a sanctuary arose, I repeat, from the position accorded to the people in virtue of the covenant, and it was the sanctuary that created the need for a priest. Priesthood has no place until a sinner has reached the position of blessing prefigured by Exodus xxiv.; and this is a position to which, under the religious system to which I refer, the sinner can never attain on earth. The truth should be clearly recognised that a place of worship and a priest are only for the *redeemed*— for those to whom Christ is made both righteousness and sanctification.

---

[1] Exodus xxiv. 5.

Here mark again the perfect accuracy of the types as key-pictures of Christian truth. It was, as we have seen, when Moses, the mediator of the covenant, after making purification for sins, went up to God, that Aaron was appointed priest.[1] And it was when the Mediator of the New Covenant, having made purification for sins, went up to the right hand of the Majesty on high, that He was "named of God" High Priest.[2] His priesthood began after His ascension. For outside the tribe of Levi there can be no earthly priesthood. So inviolable is this rule that it is said even of Christ Himself, " On earth, He would not be a priest at all." [3] That the Lord's priesthood dated from the ascension is clear. "To-day have I begotten Thee," refers not to Bethlehem, but to the resurrection.[4]

Our English word " priest " is sometimes used as a synonym for " presbyter "; and buildings in which Christians meet are called "places of worship." But conventional expressions of this

---

[1] Exodus xxiv. 8, 13; xxviii. 1. The intervening chapters deal altogether with the Tabernacle.

[2] Hebrews i. 3; v. 10.

[3] Hebrews viii. 4 (R.V.).

[4] Hebrews iv. 14; v. 5, 10.

kind must not be allowed to dim our apprehension of Divine realities. For the Christian there can be but one priest,[1] and one place of worship, namely, the Lord Jesus Christ, and "the true tabernacle which the Lord has pitched, and not man." What constitutes a place of worship in this true sense is, not that people use it as a place of meeting, but that God dwells there.

To this was due the unique sanctity and glory of the temple in Jerusalem. And yet apostate Judaism needed to be reminded that their temple was but a "shadow" of something higher and greater. "For the Most High dwelleth not in temples made with hands," as the inspired words of Solomon's dedicatory prayer, might have reminded them. "Hear Thou in heaven, Thy dwelling-place," was his oft-repeated petition, after "the glory of the Lord had filled the house of God," that house which he had "built for His dwelling for ever."

The Tabernacle and the Temple prefigured that true sanctuary to which the believer now has

---

[1] "The only priests under the Gospel, designated as such in the New Testament, are the saints, the members of the Christian brotherhood. As individuals all Christians are priests alike."—BISHOP LIGHTFOOT, *Philippians.*

access, and in which Christ fulfils His priestly ministry at the throne of God. And, as the Holy Spirit expressly warns us, access to that "Holiest of all" is incompatible with the existence of an earthly shrine.[1]

But someone will demand, perhaps, Is not the Divine presence promised wherever His people are gathered together in His Name? Most assuredly. But this only serves to confirm the truth here urged. For no virtue attaches to the *place* of gathering. Wherever His people meet in that Name, whether it be in a stately cathedral or in an "upper room," or in some retreat by a river-side, "where prayer is wont to be made," access "to the holiest" is assured to them, and "the holiest" is their true place of worship. Christianity, as Bishop Lightfoot, of Durham, wrote, "has no sacred days or seasons, no special sanctuaries, because every time and every place alike are holy."

And the words which follow deserves equal prominence. Still speaking of Christianity he adds :— "Above all it has no sacerdotal system. It interposes no sacrificial tribe or class between God

---

[1] Hebrews ix. 8.

and man, by whose intervention alone God is reconciled and man forgiven. Each individual member holds personal communion with the Divine Head. To Him immediately he is responsible, and from Him directly he obtains pardon and draws strength." [1]

God's Provision for the Way

"He is able also to save them to the uttermost that come unto God by Him."

Hebrews 7:25.

4

GOD'S PROVISION FOR THE WAY

THE twenty-fourth chapter of Exodus, though almost entirely ignored in the theology of Christendom, holds a large and prominent place in the theology of the New Testament. Indeed, it is the key to the exposition of the Epistle to the Hebrews, for it supplies the framework on which the doctrine of that Epistle rests. For the Epistle to the Hebrews has not to do with the *redemption* of the sinner, as redemption is popularly understood, but with the life and service and worship of a sinner already redeemed. The Passover, therefore, has no place in its teaching.[1] It takes up the typical story of redemption, not at the twelfth chapter of Exodus, but at the twenty-fourth. And the twenty-fourth chapter is expressly quoted or referred to again and again throughout.[2]

And one lesson of principal importance which we learn from the Epistle to the Hebrews is that,

---

[1] The historical reference in chapter xi. 28 does not affect this.

[2] See, *ex. gr.*, chapters i. 3; ix. 18-20; x. 29; xii. 29; xiii. 12, 20.

in all that follows the twenty-fourth chapter, the teaching is in part by *contrast*. The redemption sacrifices were offered " once for all." The great blood-shedding by which the Covenant was dedicated and the people were sanctified was never repeated. Neither was the Passover. For here we must distinguish between the redemption in Egypt and the yearly commemoration of that redemption. But, with one notable exception, repetition was a prominent characteristic of the sacrifices of *the law*. They foreshadowed the great sacrifice which should put away sin. But the repetition of them bore testimony that they had no real efficacy. Sin was not, in fact, put away ; " For it is impossible that the blood of bulls and goats should take away sins."

The words last quoted refer expressly to the annual sin-offering of the great Day of Atonement ; and the rite is one which claims special notice here. The ritual of it is unfolded in the sixteenth chapter of Leviticus ; and for our present purpose we may confine our attention to some of the principal features of the sin-offering for the whole congregation. In the case of the leper's cleansing, *two* sparrows were required ; and so also here, *two* kids were needed for the offering. Of these, one was killed, and its blood was sprinkled in the most holy place. The ritual respecting the other victim is thus described : " And Aaron shall lay both his hands upon the head of the live goat, and confess over him all the iniquities of the children of Israel, and all their transgressions, even all their sins ; and he shall put them upon the head of the goat, and shall send him away by the hand of a man that is in readiness into the wilderness ; and the goat shall bear upon him all their iniquities unto a solitary land." [1]

In the case of ordinary sin-offerings the laying on of hands was followed by the victim's being led away to the slaughter. We may presume, therefore, that in the symbolism of the chapter the " solitary land " represents death. And the fulfilment of this is not doubtful. " The Lord hath laid on Him the iniquity of us all." [2] " His own self bare our sins in His own body on the tree." [3]

But who are they that are thus blest ? The neglect of systematic study of the types has led to much confusion of thought, and not a little serious

---

[1] Leviticus xvi. 21, 22, R.V.
[2] Isaiah liii. 6.   [3] 1 Peter ii. 24.

error, in regard to the truth of what is called "the simple Gospel." The sin-offering, as we have seen, was only for the covenant people;[1] and if, ignoring the redemption sacrifices, we give to this an exclusive prominence, we shall limit the efficacy of the death of Christ, and leave no room for grace. The sins borne by the victim were the sins which had been confessed over its head; and the laying on of hands betokened identification with it. The offerer became identified with the victim, and the victim died in his stead. The efficacy of the death was thus strictly limited; it could neither be extended nor transferred. Therefore it is that, in Scripture, the Gospel for the unsaved is never stated in the language of the sin-offering.

But in the case of the Passover there was no laying on of hands, no preceding identification of the sinner with the sacrifice. The victim died, and it was by the sprinkling of its blood that the efficacy of its death accrued to the sinner. Just as the protection of the "scarlet line" in Jericho was extended to all the household of Rahab, and to all who came within her doors,[2] so in Egypt a believing Egyptian might have sought the shelter

---

[1] But see note, p. 27, *ante.*   [2] Joshua ii. 18, 19.

of the blood. It is not that the Passover was the revelation of *grace*—for "Grace *came by Jesus Christ*"—but it foreshadowed it. The Gospel is to be preached to every creature. " Forgiveness of sins" is proclaimed to all, without distinction; and "all that believe are justified." But they whose Gospel is limited to the Passover can know nothing of oneness with the Sinbearer; nothing of the Divine provision for the wilderness journey with all its difficulties and perils.

But what if the redeemed sinner fall by the way? Will not sin thrust him back again under Egyptian bondage, and create the need for a new redemption? Most emphatically, *No*. Sin might bring Israel to Babylon; but a return to Egypt was for ever barred.[1] The only sin for which there can be no forgiveness is the sin of apostasy from Christ and "doing despite" unto the Spirit of grace.[2] It is an "*eternal* redemption" that Christ has obtained.[3]

The new theology makes so light of sin that the question here raised scarcely concerns it. And the old theology, owing to its neglect of the types,

---

[1] Deuteronomy xvii. 16.
[2] Hebrews x. 26–29, *cf*. Mark iii. 29.   [3] Hebrews ix. 12,

gives an answer which is inadequate. When the Israelite sinned he brought his sin-offering. It was the definite acknowledgment (or " confession ") of his sin, and it obtained for him forgiveness. But as we have seen, a sinner needs more than forgiveness, for God is holy. He must have a twofold cleansing, and this was provided for in the ritual of the great Day of Expiation. His sins were laid upon the head of the scapegoat. And further, atonement was made by the blood of the slaughtered victim, carried within the vail and sprinkled on the mercy-seat. Thus were the benefits accruing both from the Passover and from the Burnt-offering of the Covenant renewed and continued to the Israelite.

And we have this twofold cleansing in the opening chapter of the First Epistle of John. The blood upon the mercy-seat cleanses us from all sin. "And if we confess our sins, He is faithful and just . . . to cleanse us from all unrighteousness." Sin is thus dealt with in a twofold aspect. Nor is this all, for the word is added; "*If any man sin*, we have an Advocate with the Father, Jesus Christ the righteous ; and He is the propitiation for our sins."[1]

---

[1] 1 John i. 7–9; ii. 1, 2.

In dealing with truth like this, we need to keep closely to the very words of Scripture. When we say that Christ has made atonement or propitiation, we use the language of theology. According to the passage last cited (and the statement is repeated in chapter iv. 10) He *is* the propitiation. In our English Bible a similar statement occurs in Romans iii. 25 ; but the term there used is different; and our rendering of it, if not erroneous, is at least inadequate. Of Christ it is said, "Whom God set forth to be a *mercy-seat* through faith in His blood." It was by virtue of the blood of atonement that the cover of the Ark was the mercy-seat—the place where God and the sinner could meet. And it is because of His death on Calvary that the Lord Jesus Christ is both the mercy-seat and the propitiation.

The "merits" of the scapegoat were, as we have seen, strictly limited to those whose sins had been confessed upon its head. But if a heathen stranger, on hearing of the holiness and terribleness of the Jehovah God who "dwelt between the cherubim," demanded whether it were safe to sojourn in the camp of Israel, he would have been told of the blood-sprinkled mercy-seat.

For the atonement of the mercy-seat was for all. And so, to the words already cited—"He is the propitiation for our sins"—the Holy Spirit adds, "And not for ours only, *but also for the whole world*."

Treating the words "atonement" and "propitiation" thus as synonyms is a concession to theology. And yet strict accuracy in our phraseology is most important. Indeed, no amount of accuracy can be excessive; nor need we shrink from insisting on it, in spite of the censures or the sneers of "superior persons." For while the use of the literary microscope is deemed "scholarship" and "modern criticism"—provided our purpose be to discredit Scripture—it becomes "hyper-criticism" and "hair-splitting" if we thus seek to bring out the hidden harmony of Scripture, and to establish its truth and accuracy.

And no scholarship is needed to enable us to mark the kinship between words that are closely related, or to appreciate the significance of a change of terms.

The propitiation is *hilasmos*. This word occurs only in 1 John ii. 2, and iv. 10.

The propitiatory, or mercy-seat, is *hilastērion*,

which word is used only in Romans iii. 25, and Hebrews ix. 5.

To make propitiation is *hilaskomai*, a word that occurs only in Luke xviii. 13 (" be merciful "), and Hebrews ii. 17.

As appears from the second passage, where this last word is used, making propitiation is a part of our Lord's present priestly work for His people. The rendering of our Authorised Version is unfortunate; for the phrase " making reconciliation " is elsewhere used to represent a wholly different Greek word.[1] And the confusion is increased by rendering the kindred noun of this other word as " atonement " in Romans v. 11. Christ *is* the Propitiation, and as a continuing work He makes propitiation. But reconciliation is a work past and finished.

In his " Synonyms of the New Testament," Archbishop Trench brackets " redemption " with these two words, " reconciliation " and " propitiation "; and the opening passage of his treatise respecting them may fitly close this chapter. He writes :—

" There are three grand circles of images, by

---

[1] *Katallassō*; used in Romans v. and 2 Corinthians v.; and in an intensified form in Ephesians ii. 16 and Colossians i. 20, 21.

aid of which it is sought in the Scriptures of the New Testament to set forth to us the inestimable benefits of Christ's death and passion. Transcending, as these benefits do, all human thought, and failing to find anywhere a perfectly adequate expression in human language, they must still be set forth by the help of language, and through the means of human relations. Here, as in other similar cases, what the Scripture does is to approach the central truth from different quarters; to seek to set it forth not on one side but on many, that so these may severally supply the deficiency of one another, and that moment of the truth which one does not express, another may. The words placed at the head of this article, *apolutrōsis,* or redemption; *katallagē,* or reconciliation; *hilasmos,* or propitiation, are the capital words summing up three such families of images, to one or other of which almost every word directly bearing on this work of our salvation through Christ may be more or less remotely referred."

Recognizing My Need

"Lord, if Thou wilt, Thou canst make me clean. And He put forth His hand, and touched him, saying, I will; be thou clean. And immediately the leprosy departed from him."

Luke 5:12,13.

5

RECOGNIZING MY NEED

THE ordinances of the Mosaic code formed part of the ordinary law of the Commonwealth of Israel. Owing to our ignorance of the "local colouring," and of the circumstances to which they were adapted, we are often unable to appreciate, sometimes even to understand them. But not a few of them had a typical and spiritual significance ; they were "a shadow of the coming good things." The law of the leper is an instance of this ; and it will usefully serve as a recapitulation of much that has been put forward in preceding chapters.

As with the parables, so also with the types ; intelligence is needed in deducing the spiritual lessons they are meant to teach. In neither case should we force a meaning upon every detail. But the main outlines are always clear. In the symbolism of Scripture the connection between leprosy and sin is not doubtful. And what first commands our attention here is that it was the fact of the disease, which entitled the sufferer to the services of those who were Divinely appointed to deal with it. The fact of his sin is the sinner's sufficient warrant for coming to the Saviour.

And the next fact is still more striking. It is stated thus :—" If the leprosy cover all the skin of him that hath the plague from his head even to his foot, wheresoever the priest looketh . . . he shall pronounce him clean that hath the plague." [1]

If we dissemble and cloak our sins, we need not look for mercy. Divine forgiveness is for sinners *as such*. " Truth springeth out of the earth, and righteousness hath looked down from heaven." [2] And the only truth which God requires from the sinner is the acknowledgment of what he

---

[1] Leviticus xiii. 12, 13. The objection urged by Edersheim, that modern medical science would not accept the disease here described as leprosy, does not affect what I have here written. The ordinance was for a primitive people in primitive circumstances, and the language of the passage above quoted leaves no doubt whatever that the disease was to be *treated* as leprosy. Language, indeed, could not be plainer. We have a precise parallel to this in England at the present time. As a mild case of small-pox is sometimes mistaken for chicken-pox, it is proposed that this comparatively harmless disease shall be brought under the law which requires all small-pox cases to be reported and isolated. Nothing, moreover, in Edersheim's criticisms can affect the *typical* significance of the passage and of the rites unfolded in it.

[2] Psalm lxxxv. 11, R.V.

is. " Faithful is the saying, and worthy of all acceptation, that Christ Jesus came into the world to save sinners." And with this confession of Christ must be joined the confession of *sin* : and that must be in the spirit of the Apostle's words, " of whom I am chief." No false pleas based on supposed piety or penitence will avail ; no pretence of being anything, or of having anything, to create a special claim for pardon. What God demands of us is *truth*—the self-abasement of the full and unqualified acknowledgment of what we are.

A man who pleads his piety or his penitence is like a candidate for admission to an asylum for the pauper blind, who borrows good clothes to hide his poverty, and coloured spectacles to conceal his blindness. Such was the spirit of the Pharisee's plea. And every student of human nature, knows that the publican could have made out as plausible a case as the Pharisee. But he, taking his true place, cast himself unreservedly upon Divine mercy : " God, be merciful to me, a sinner." [1] " *The* sinner " was what he really said. England has three-score gaols full of prisoners ; but in a criminal court the prisoner in the dock

---

[1] Luke xviii. 13.

is *the* prisoner. And such is the thought here : such, the position of every one who really comes to the Cross.

The leper's habitation, we read, was " outside the camp"; and there, with rent clothes, bared head, and a covered lip, he was to cry, " Unclean, unclean!"[1] The type thus teaches us the Divine estimate of sin. It goes on to teach how the sinner may be cleansed and "made nigh." We have already noticed the striking ordinance that if the disease turned inwards the leper was unclean, but that he was to be pronounced clean if and when the leprosy was out over all his body. For sin cloaked or unconfessed there is nothing but banishment and wrath. But for the "humble, lowly, penitent, and obedient" there is no reserve in Divine "goodness and mercy."

And mark the words, "the priest shall pronounce him clean that hath the plague." He was to pronounce the *leper* clean ; and to pronounce him *clean*. Not that he had not the plague, or that only a little of it showed ; but if and when he was covered with disease from head to foot. The common belief is that Christ Jesus came into the

---

[1] Leviticus xiii. 45.　　　 s xiii. 45.

world to save *saints*. But the right word is *sinners*. Pardon and salvation are for sinners. Not for sinners with a qualifying adjective, but for the ungodly, the guilty, and the lost. He came " to seek and to save that which was lost."

Next let us mark the time and manner of the pronouncement. One of the birds was to be killed, and its blood sprinkled on the leper. Death thus passed upon him ; for such is always the meaning of blood-sprinkling. The priest was then to take the live bird, and dipping it in the blood of the dead bird—thus identifying it with the dead bird—to let it loose as he uttered the word " clean." We now understand why two birds were needed to bring out all the truth. The Lord Jesus Christ " was delivered for our offences, and was raised again for our justification " ;[1] and the release of the live bird was the public fact which proved to the leper that he was clean. The resurrection of Christ is the public proof that sin has been put away.

Not that the leper *felt* he was clean, nor that the sinner *feels* he is forgiven. Some time since, an article appeared in *The Fortnightly Review* to

[1] Romans iv. 25.

prove that the feelings which usually accompany conversion may be produced by inhaling "laughing-gas." And feelings, however produced, may be transient. But it is not on feelings that the believer rests, but on Divine facts, declared and attested by "the living and eternally abiding Word of God."

A man who is content with "feeling happy" is a fool. Laughing-gas or opium will give him that feeling. And "peace in *believing*" is no better, unless what we believe is fact and truth. Men have been happy and at peace in believing that they were wealthy, when all the time their peace and happiness were due to ignorance of a disaster that had made them paupers. And the newspapers lately told the sad story of a man who killed himself to escape from the misery of dire poverty at the very time when he was being advertised for to inherit a fortune. What a parable to illustrate the case of "anxious sinners," who hug their misery while the Gospel is the Divine advertisement that a fortune awaits their acceptance of it!

Receiving His Provision

"Ye are clean through the word which I have spoken unto you."

John 15:3.

6

RECEIVING HIS PROVISION

IN the preceding chapters there are passages
which may lead someone to ask despairingly
whether a sinner's pardon depends on his master-
ing the theology of the Gospel as there unfolded.
And the question claims an answer.

"The Word was with God, and the Word was
God, . . . and without Him was not anything
made that was made." We cannot think too
highly of the glorious Majesty of Him who was
"the Mighty God, the Everlasting Father, the
Prince of Peace." And yet, during His ministry
on earth, He was within reach of the poorest and
the worst of men, and " as many as touched Him
were made perfectly whole." So in the type, " two
sparrows," to be had for a farthing, were the
leper's appointed offering. [1] Our salvation depends
on the Lord Jesus Christ; not on the measure of

---
[1] Leviticus xiv. 4 (*marg.*).

our appreciation of Him. The slenderest wire
may suffice to convey the current which floods our
room with light. Not that there is any light in
the wire itself. There is no merit in faith; yet
the faith which, as it were, but touches the hem
of His garment " makes the connection " which
brings Divine light into the soul.

The farthing offering availed to introduce the
outcast leper into the citizenship of the camp of
Israel; but much more than this was expected of
him as a citizen. He was then to bring all the
great offerings of the law, every one of which
typified some special aspect of the work of Christ.
While " a farthing Gospel " will bring forgiveness, and make the sinner nigh, grace has failed
of its due effect on him, if, as forgiven and
made nigh, he is content with this. His new
blessedness will create new desires and needs
which Christ in all His fulness alone can
satisfy.

In the seventh verse of Leviticus xiv. the leper
is pronounced clean, and yet in the next and
following verses he is spoken of as " he that is
to be cleansed." But there is no inconsistency
in this. It is analogous to the completion of

the Passover redemption by the burnt-offering of the covenant: analogous to the double cleansing of 1 John i. 7 and 9.

Indeed there is a third cleansing here (verse 8); and it claims prominent notice. The offering gave *ceremonial* cleansing, but *practical* cleanness also was required. The leper was to wash himself. Washing by blood was one of the rites of pagan cults which had such a sinister influence upon the Church of the Fathers; but in Scripture—Old Testament and New, alike—washing is only and always by water, and its significance is only and always practical clearing ourselves from evil. Revelation i. 5, and vii. 14 may seem to clash with this; but in the one passage the right reading is "loosed us from our sins."[1] And in the other, a right reading is popularly misread. It is "they washed their robes, and they made them white in the blood of the Lamb." The "righteous acts" of the saints are the fine linen of their robes.[2] But apart from Christ "all our righteousnesses (or righteous acts) are filthy rags." It is the blood

---

[1] See R.V. In the "Received Text" *louo* is used in error for *luo*.

[2] Revelation xix. 8, R.V.

that sanctifies which alone can make them "clean and white." [1]

So in the First Epistle to the Corinthians, the Apostle Paul, after enumerating the sins and vices of their former life, adds words which our English versions, misunderstanding their symbolic meaning, have misread. "But," he writes, "you washed yourselves, but you were sanctified, but you were justified, in the name of the Lord Jesus Christ, and in the Spirit of our God." [2]

And mark where the washing came in the ritual of the leper's cleansing. It was before his admission to the camp, but after the offering of the

---

[1] This may account for the two readings of Revelation xxii. 14, "Blessed are they that wash their robes" (R.V.). "Blessed are they that do His commandments" (A.V.). The reading of the "Received Text" is probably a gloss introduced by someone who understood the meaning of the figure, "washed their robes."

[2] See R.V. (*margin*) of 1 Corinthians vi. 11. As Alford writes: "The 1 aor. mid. cannot by any possibility be passive in signification, as it is generally, for doctrinal reasons, here rendered." Albeit both here and in Acts xxii. 16 (the only other place where *apolouo* occurs) Alford, *more suo*, refers it to baptism. The amazing theory that a sinner washes away his sins by going down into the water of baptism is borrowed from the cults of classic paganism. (See Dr. Hatch's *Hibbert Lectures*, 1888). But the inspired words of Ananias, recorded in Acts xxii. 16, had reference not to the Eleusinian mysteries, but to the typology of Holy Scripture, and they might be paraphrased thus—"Arise, and be baptized, and lead a new life, calling on the name of the Lord."

birds, after the sprinkling of the blood, and after the priest had pronounced him clean. Here is a great truth which men will not have, though God enforces it in ways unnumbered. There can be no recognition of good works or of amendment of life, and no citizenship with the saints, until after the sinner has, as a sinner, accepted Christ.

At this point the teaching of the type is of the highest practical importance. The Gospel is sometimes presented in such a way as to convey the impression that a cleansed life is of no account, and that Christ will receive sinners on their own terms. Others, again, in ignorance of grace, plainly assert that sinners must turn from the practice of their sins *before* they come to Him. But indulgence in sinful practices so degrades a man that after a time all power of recovery is gone. The drunkard, for example, will turn to the bottle, and the impure to his immoralities, no matter what the consequences. And is there no salvation for such? Most assuredly there is. If a man says, " I *will not* give up my sins," then indeed we must act as Moses did in the case of the sinner who "blasphemed the Name"—we must turn away and wait upon God. But to the poor wretch who says, "*I cannot*," it is our high privilege and duty to tell of a Saviour who is "mighty to save."

Just as there was cleansing for a leper *as a leper*, so there is salvation for a drunkard *as a drunkard*, for the sensualist *as a sensualist*. To make it a condition of pardon that men shall first extricate themselves from the horrible pit and the miry clay, is to deny grace altogether. It is utterly false. We cannot exaggerate the grace of God. But while the true minister of Christ, will preach a Gospel that will reach the lost sinner, no matter how far he is gone in sin, he will enjoin upon the believing sinner to "wash himself," nor will he forget about the sin-offering, and the burnt-offering, and the meat-offering.

The leper, as we have seen, experienced a two-fold cleansing by blood. The blood of the dead bird was sprinkled upon him, and afterwards the blood of the trespass-offering was placed upon his head and hand and foot, sanctifying every part of his person. And then, *upon the blood*, was put the anointing oil.[1] This foreshadows the theology of the New Testament. Christ is made to the

[1] Leviticus xiv. 18.　　　　xiv. 18.

sinner both justification and sanctification—the sinner is justified by blood and sanctified by blood —and this full redemption is inseparable from the Spirit's work. But Christ is *first*. The oil was put upon the blood, not the blood upon the oil. It is idle for the sinner to claim the Spirit's presence or influence until, as a sinner, he comes to Christ. The witness of the Spirit to sonship is only for the believer. His witness to the person and work of Christ is for every sinner who, as a sinner, hears "the word of the truth of the Gospel."

What a costly and elaborate ritual it was! "Two he-lambs without blemish, and one ewe-lamb of the first year without blemish, and three tenths deals of flour, and one log of oil."[1] I have already sought to quiet the fears of some poor outsider coming to the Cross: and here, perchance, some earnest, true-hearted believer may shrink back dismayed, exclaiming, "All this is above me! I can't rise to it, I am too poor." For such I would emphasize the words that follow— "And if he be poor, and cannot get so much," the chapter goes on to say, then let him bring

---

[1] Leviticus xiv. 10.

one lamb and a pair of pigeons. And even this is qualified by the added words : " Such as he can get—even such as he is able to get." [1] How infinite " the kindness and love-toward-man of our Saviour God " ! [2]

I heard a story long ago of a poor, half-witted creature, known to everybody in a certain town as " Silly Billy," a harmless wight and devout withal in his own simple way. One day he was found in a conclave where " the wise and prudent " were discussing the doctrine of the Trinity ; and to the amusement of some, he appeared to be taking notes. In a bantering way they asked to see his " notes " ; and on the scrap of paper he produced, they found these words :—

> " This can Silly Billy see,
>   Three in One and One in Three,
>   And One of them has died for me."

Here was the poor fellow's creed—his " such as he was able to get." And his " two mites that make a farthing " were possibly more acceptable to God than the seeming abundance of some of the wise and prudent. For with God the test

---

[1] Leviticus xiv. 21, 30, 31,

[2] Titus iii, 4.

is, " According to that a man hath, and not according to that he hath not." [1]

But there must be "first the willing mind." For " God is not mocked." His grace is infinite to the humble and contrite, and to such as tremble at His Word. But ignorance begotten of indolence and wilful neglect of His Word, grace will not condone. And ignorance due to sheer contempt of His Word, calls only for judgment. If these Books of Moses, God-given as a picture alphabet of the language in which the full revelation of Christianity is written, are despised as a farrago of old-word legends and priestly frauds, what room can there be for grace? "Fools and blind" were epithets which the Lord reserved for men who, while boasting of superior enlightenment, were leading others into the ditch. For the poor and needy, the erring and the weak, He had infinite compassion.

In closing, I would notice that while the ritual for the leper's cleansing was an eight days' business, the Gospel brings fulness of blessing to the sinner on believing. This is one of the characteristic differences between law and grace.

---

[1] 2 Corinthians viii. 12.

And, further, that the value of these ordinances as key-pictures of Christian truth, is greatly enhanced just because the several steps are so definitely marked. We are thus taught to seek, in the great reality of the redemption that is ours in Christ, for the fulfilment of every part.

And though there is no chronological sequence in the believer's reception of these benefits, for all that Christ is to the sinner becomes his when he receives Him, there is none the less a moral order, as the teaching of the types so plainly indicates. And the ignoring of this has led not only to error but to strife. As we have already seen, the sin-offering does not precede, but follows the redemption sacrifices; and so in the law of the leper's cleansing, it comes after his restoration to the camp.

Justification and Sanctification
Through Redemption

"Of Him are ye in Christ Jesus, who was made unto us wisdom from God, and both righteousness and sanctification, even redemption."

1 Corinthians 1:30, R.V., marg., see p. 36 footnote 2.

7

JUSTIFICATION AND SANCTIFICATION
THROUGH REDEMPTION

A CONVERSATION with a brother barrister one morning long ago brought very vividly before my mind the difference between the theology of Christendom and the truth of Christ on the doctrine of Justification. My friend began by taking me to task for preaching. He charged me with "usurping apostolic functions." Having my Testament at hand, I showed him from Acts viii. that, in the Stephen persecution, the Jerusalem Christians "were all scattered abroad, *except the Apostles*," and that "they that were scattered abroad went everywhere preaching the Word." The Apostles, therefore, were the only Christians who did not, at that time, go out preaching.

Baffled and silenced on this point, he tried to make a diversion by declaiming against Protestant misrepresentations of his Church's teaching, for he was a Roman Catholic. "You think," he said, "that we believe in salvation by works, whereas the Church teaches salvation through Christ. But

Christ died for the whole world. How is it, then, that some are saved and others not? The Church and good works merely put people into the right position to get saved through Christ."

To which I replied, "There is one great truth of Christianity of which your Church knows absolutely nothing."

" What is that?" he asked.

"Justification by grace," I answered.

" You mean justification *by faith*," said he.

" No," I said, " I mean justification *by grace*."

After a little fencing, he told me plainly that he did not understand me; and, with frequent interruptions on his part, I went on to explain what I meant.[1]

Between justification by faith and salvation by works, as explained by my friend, there is, in theory at least, no necessary antagonism. But the whole position is absolutely inconsistent with justification by grace. For if a sinner has a claim of any kind for blessing or mercy, there is no room

---

[1] This occurred shortly before I gave up Court practice at the Bar. Several years afterwards I resumed the conversation with my friend by asking him if he still stood where he did when we used to meet in Court. His answer was, " No, I am now a member of the Evangelical party of the Church of England."

for grace. Therefore it was that grace could not be revealed till Christ came. Till then, men held relationships with God, based either on creation, or on covenant, or on promise. But relationships are in their very nature two-sided; and as the Cross of Christ outraged every claim which God had upon man, it destroyed every claim which man had upon God. The whole world now stands on a common level of sin and wrath. For neither Church, nor sacrament, nor personal effort, can avail to establish a difference, since God has declared that there is *no* difference. The Cross has levelled all distinctions, and shut men up to judgment; this is the dark background on which "the grace of God, salvation-bringing to all men, has been manifested." [1]

And the grace of God is not, as some seem to think, a kind of good influence imparted to the sinner to fit him to receive Divine blessing. It is the principle on which God blesses sinners in whom He can find no fitness whatsoever. And grace has now been *manifested*. In the Old Testament it was implied, indeed, but veiled;

---

[1] Titus ii. 11, R.V., *revised*; for "bringing salvation" may be misread. The word is an adjective, not a verb.

in the New, it is an open revelation. Grace was behind the promises. But neither in the case of God nor of man, is it grace *to fulfil* a promise. There is no grace in bestowing favour upon one who has a claim to favour, whether that claim depend upon promise or upon relationship. But when men became " the betrayers and murderers " of the Son of God, every promise was forfeited, every relationship sacrificed; sin reached its climax, and a lost world was shut up to judgment, stern, relentless, and terrible.

But now, judgment waits on grace. For all judgment has been committed to the Son; and He has been " exalted to be a Prince and a Saviour, to give repentance and remission of sins." An amnesty has been proclaimed, and during this day of grace the judgment throne is empty. GRACE is reigning through righteousness unto eternal life, by our Lord Jesus Christ.[1]

The sinner, then, is "justified by grace," because God can find no reason, no motive, save in His own heart, for blessing him at all.

He is "justified by faith," because this is the only principle of blessing consistent with grace.

---

[1] John v. 24; Acts v. 31 (*cf.* xi. 18); Romans v. 21.

And, thirdly, he is "justified by blood," because the stern facts of Divine righteousness and human sin make blessing impossible, save on the ground of redemption.

And justification by blood is to be explained, not by the rites of ancient paganism, but by the teaching of the Divine religion of the Old Testament. For Scripture must be interpreted by Scripture. This caution is needed; for some men speak of the blood in such a way as to provoke the taunt that Christianity is "a religion of the shambles." In the symbolism of Scripture, "blood" means death *applied*. Therefore it is that we are said to be justified by the *blood* of Christ. Were it said to be "by His death," it would be true of every child of Adam. Such, therefore, is its scope in Romans v. 18, where the justification has reference to what theologians call "original sin." As wide as are the effects of Adam's "one offence," no less wide are the effects of that "'one righteous act,' the death of Christ viewed as the acme of His obedience."[1]

The distinction here noticed is very marked in the ninth and tenth verses of this same chapter.

---

[1] Dean Alford *in loco*.

The "justification" is, as we have seen, by the *blood* of Christ, for it is only for those who by faith become one with Him in His death. But "reconciliation" is by *His death*, for reconciliation was accomplished at the Cross, and is "received" by the sinner on believing.[1]

And the believer is not only justified, but sanctified, and on the same ground. Sanctification by blood is a lost truth. Not only in popular preaching and teaching, but even in our standard theology, the verb "to sanctify" is generally used to express only a progressive change in the Christian's life; and yet it is never once so used in the New Testament.[2]

Christ is made unto us both righteousness and sanctification; and the Corinthians, to whom these words are written, are addressed by the Apostle as "them that are sanctified in Christ Jesus, called saints." Not "called *to be* saints," but saints by their calling. To become a saint is the

---

[1] Verse 11.—The word here is *reconciliation*, not "atonement." It includes not only this world of ours, but the whole universe of God (Colossians i. 20).

[2] 1 Thessalonians v. 23 may seem an exception to this; but the word "wholly" there refers not to the completion of a process, but to the completeness of a man as including "spirit, soul, and body."

effort of the religionist; but the redeemed sinner is a saint in virtue of his redemption. The struggle of the religionist is to become *what he is not*; the aim of the Christian is to realize *what he is*—to " walk worthy of the calling wherewith he is called." " Saints and sinners " is an ignorant and false antithesis; for every saint is a sinner, though every sinner is not a saint.

The Reformation has taught us how false is the teaching of the religion of Christendom as to justification; but seemingly we have yet to learn that its doctrine of sanctification is no less erroneous. The Divine grace which freely justifies a sinner, and then teaches him to live righteously, also sanctifies and teaches him to live holily. He does not live righteously in order to become justified, but because he has been justified; neither does he live holily in order to become sanctified, but because he has been sanctified.

And as he is justified, so also is he sanctified, by the blood of Christ. Or, to drop the language of the types, when the sinner, on his believing on the Lord Jesus Christ, becomes one with Him in His death, " the merits " of that death are his, and he stands before God both righteous and holy in Christ. This is not a mystical theory, but a glorious Divine fact. And in keeping with it, "saint" is the characteristic title usually given to the Christian in the Epistles.

And as with justification and sanctification, so also with redemption. "The redemption of the world" is a theological expression which has no sanction in Scripture. Most true it is that Christ "gave Himself a ransom for *all*"; but redemption includes not merely the payment of the ransom but the deliverance of the ransomed. Hence the language of Scripture, "In whom we have redemption *through His blood*." Not that we would set limits to the Gospel of the Grace of God. That Gospel is "preached in all creation under heaven."[1] The great amnesty is for all. But while the reconciliation of the world is a Divine truth, the redemption is only for those who "have received the reconciliation."

But this is somewhat in the nature of a digression, for salvation by grace is here my theme. And there is no truth which the natural man,

[1] Colossians i. 23, R.V.

whether Christian or pagan, so resents. If "there is no difference" in God's sight between one man and another, what is the use of "religion"? The Pharisee is in as bad a case.as the publican. Yes, so it is. Indeed, the Book says he is in a worse case. Not because there is any merit in the publican, but because he acknowledges his condition and throws himself on Divine mercy.

If, as in effect Paul said to the Athenians, men would but use their brains, they would undei stand that the God "who made the world and all things therein" cannot stoop to receive anything from men.[1] He is the One who *gives*. But the great GIVER is "the unknown God"— unknown not only to Athenian idolaters but to multitudes who call themselves Christians.

A lady of my acquaintance, well known in the higher ranks of London society, called upon me one day to ask for police help, to relieve her from certain annoyances. Her evident distress at my inability to give her the protection she sought, led me to remark that the peace of God in the heart was a great antidote to trouble.

---

[1] Acts xvii. 23–25.

" Ah," said she, " if I was only like you ! " " If it depended on merit," I replied with real sincerity, " it is you who would have the peace, not I." Presently her manner changed, and with tears in her eyes she told me something of her spiritual struggles. If she could be more earnest, more devout, more prayerful, she was sure that God would accept her.

" I was greatly interested," I remarked, " by what I heard about the supper you gave the tramps last week. Did they offer you anything for it ? Of course, they had no money, but they might have brought you some of their coats or shirts."

" If you had only seen their coats and shirts ! " she exclaimed with a smile.

" Filthy rags they were, I'm sure," said I, " and what you don't believe is that in God's sight 'all our *righteousnesses* are as filthy rags !' "

But no ; people will not believe it. And so they put from them the blessing that awaits every sinner who believes in the Lord Jesus Christ. " For by grace are ye saved, through faith," the Gospel declares.

" Faith, yes; we must get faith "; this is the

very last plank to which the sinner clings in his struggle to assert himself in some way. What good works are to the Roman Catholic religionist, faith is to the Protestant: not, of course, a ground of salvation, but a means by which a sinner can raise himself above the common level, and thus obtain the good offices of the Saviour. But "it is of faith, that it may be *by grace*."[1] Faith is not something which the sinner gives to God, but merely the receiving what God has got to give to him.

"By grace are ye saved, through faith." But error is so insidious and so vital that the Scripture does not stop at a positive statement of the truth, but adds the words, "and that (salvation) not of yourselves, it is the gift of God; not of works, lest any man should boast."

To speak of *earning* a gift would be a contradiction in terms; but though a gift can not be earned by works, it may be *deserved* on that ground. Men's gifts, indeed, are seldom bestowed upon the undeserving. Therefore it is that they so often give ground for boasting. But salvation is not only unearned, but undeserved; it is not

[1] Romans iv. 16.

only a gift, but a gift *by grace*. And so, in the passage already cited, words are piled up to describe the sinner's ruin and doom. By nature we are—

"Children of wrath,"

"Dead in sins,"

"Without Christ,"

"Aliens from the commonwealth of Israel,"

"Strangers from the covenants of promise,"

"Having no hope,"

"And without God in the world."

And mark the contrast: "But now in Christ Jesus ye who sometimes were far off are made nigh by the blood of Christ, for He is our peace." In ourselves nothing but evil, and absolute and utter ruin; in Christ all that we can need, and all that God requires.

---

[1] Ephesians ii. 3–14.

Change of Dispensation

"The law was given by Moses; grace and truth came by Jesus Christ."

John 1:17.

8

CHANGE OF DISPENSATION

ONE evening, many years ago, when, during a summer holiday, I was holding meetings in a certain provincial town, I had an unexpected visitor. He was a medical practitioner in a neighbouring county, who had been converted the year before, and had already begun to tell the Gospel to others. He had come over, as he said, "to help me."

As we sat at tea, he began to rail at what he called "dispensational truth." I tried in vain to instruct him. I sought to show him, for example, that the death of Christ had made a change in God's relationships with men. But he would not listen. "He could not tolerate that way of cutting up the Bible, and setting one part against another." My thoughts were full of my evening meeting, and I dismissed the subject by saying that ignorance of "dispensational truth" would embarrass him in Gospel work.

In addressing the meeting he took Luke xiv.
16, 17, as his text, and with much iteration and
earnestness he pressed upon the hearers that they
were bidden to the great supper, and warned them
against rejecting or neglecting the invitation. In
conclusion, he read the following verses, one by
one, commenting on each in turn. But when he
came to the twenty-fourth—"I say unto you, that
none of those men that were bidden shall taste of
my supper," he naturally became confused; and at
last, turning round to look at me, he collapsed
altogether.

I rose immediately, and, identifying myself with
the spirit of his words, I explained that, as with
many another sermon, *the text* was wrong. The
mission of Christ was primarily to the covenant
people. "I am not sent but to the lost sheep of
the house of Israel;" "It is not meet to take the
children's bread and to cast it to dogs;" "He
came unto *His own*, but His own received Him
not." As the parable tells us, the bidden guests—
the favoured people—made light of the invitation;
and now, outcast sinners are called in—the waifs
and paupers of "the streets and lanes of the city."

I have already called attention to the forgotten

truth that the Bible is the history of the covenant people. In the great drama it unfolds there is a double interlude. The New Testament opens with "The book of the generation of Jesus Christ, the Son of David, the Son of Abraham." The Davidic covenant was put in abeyance when, because of their sins, the people were brought under servitude to Babylon. And then great Gentile empires appeared upon the scene. The Abrahamic covenant in its earthly aspect was put in abeyance when Israel rejected the Messiah. But neither covenant is abandoned. He has set aside His people, but He has not finally cast them away (for the seeming contradiction between the second and fifteenth verses of the eleventh chapter of Romans arises from the wording of our English versions). And the rejection, or setting aside, of them is "the reconciliation of the world."

It is not that the world is brought within the covenant, but that grace is free to all alike. There is no difference between Jew and Gentile as to condemnation, "for all have sinned;"[1] nor yet as to mercy, "for the same Lord is Lord of all, and is rich unto all that call upon Him."[2]

---

[1] Romans iii. 22, 23.   [2] Romans x. 12, R.V.

Under the covenant the Jew had priority in blessing, but not a monopoly. The ante-diluvian apostasy was wiped out in the judgment of the Flood. The post-diluvian apostasy, which produced Babylon—the perversion of every truth in God's preceding revelations to the race—God met by making Abraham and his descendants His agents, as it were, on the earth. "Unto them were committed the oracles of God;" theirs were "the service of God, and the promises." The Jew sought to treat the agency as a monopoly; but that it was agency is clear, not merely from the New Testament, but from the Old—witness, for example, the words of the Covenant itself, or of Solomon's inspired prayer at the dedication of the Temple.

When an agent is false to his trust, the principal may change his system, and deal directly with all the world; but the suggestion that he would appoint all the world as his agents is grotesquely absurd. God has not raised the world to the position forfeited by the Jew, but He has relegated the Jew to the same level as the world.

"To the Jew first" was the characteristic of

the bygone dispensation; not "To the Jew *only*," for that was never true. "There is no difference," is the characteristic of the present dispensation. It is not that "the same Lord is rich unto *all*"—that is the false creed of one phase of the Christian apostasy—but that He is "rich unto *all that call upon Him*." "Salvation is of the Jews," the Lord Jesus Himself declared.[1] But now it is, "Whosoever shall call upon the name of the Lord shall be saved."

"Whosoever": I remember a story of Harry Moorhouse's about that word. After his first visit to the United States an American gentleman sent him a typewriter. And typewriters were scarce in those days. But he had some difficulty in obtaining delivery of it. For it appeared that he had a namesake living near him; and he was put to the strictest proof that it was for him, and not for his namesake, that the gift was intended. "I am very glad," said he, "that the Lord made it 'whosoever' in John iii. 16; for if He had put my name in the verse I never could have been sure that He didn't mean the other Harry Moorhouse!"

---

[1] John iv. 22.

But here, again, the blessing is only for "whosoever *believeth*." To suppose that the Gentile, as such, has attained to the place of favour formerly enjoyed by the Jew is sheer error. The "olive-tree" position of Romans xi. (which must not be confounded with union with Christ as "the Vine") symbolizes the place of earthly privilege and responsibility, accorded to the Church of this dispensation, the Church designed by God to be His household upon earth, the sheepfold of the sheep, the nursery and home of His people during their sojourn here. But the maintenance of the "olive" relationship by the "professing Church" was made conditional upon faith and faithfulness. And how has that condition been fulfilled? In a passage of striking solemnity and force Dean Alford deals with this subject. The parable of the cast-out demon that returns with seven others to find the house empty, he refers primarily to the Jewish people. And he adds:—

"Strikingly parallel with this runs the history of the Christian Church. Not long after the Apostolic times the golden calves of idolatry were set up. What the effect of the *Captivity* was to the Jews, that of the Reformation has been to Christendom. The first evil spirit has been cast out; but by the growth of hypocrisy, secularity, and rationalism, the house has become swept and garnished by the decencies of civilization and the discoveries of secular knowledge, but empty of living and earnest faith. And he must read prophecy but ill who does not see under all these seeming improvements the preparation for the final development of the Man of Sin, the great repossession which is to bring the outward frame of Christendom to a fearful end" (Greek Testament, Matthew xii. 44).

"The Christian Church" soon ceased to be a company of Christian people. The real Christians within it became a petty minority. And "Church and World" has ever since been a false antithesis. The Church is itself the world, in a specially subtle and evil phase. Even while His Apostles were still on earth, the Lord uttered these solemn words of warning to the Church: "I will spue thee out of my mouth."[1] And the time seems hastening on when the further word will go forth: "Come out of her, my people, that ye be

---

[1] Revelation iii. 16.

not partakers of her sins, and that ye receive not
of her plagues." [1] Meanwhile, Christians can
remain in " the professing Church." But let
them, while using their several " denominations "
in their Master's service, keep in mind the precept
about " using the world as not abusing it " (that is,
using it unduly).

In days when the historic apostasy of Christendom has well-nigh captured the National Church,
and the new infidel apostasy, hiding under the veil
of " the Higher Criticism," is leavening *all* the
churches, it behoves the Christian to " keep himself pure." For every true Christian will echo the
words of the great Dr. Chalmers : " Who cares
about any Church, but as an instrument of Christian good ? "

Have, then, the gates of hell prevailed against
the Church ? No spiritual Christian,—no man of
intelligence, indeed—can arrive at any other conclusion. " But," it will be demanded, " does not
this falsify the Lord's emphatic words ? " Most
assuredly not. When the Lord declared that the
counsels of hell should *not* prevail against His
Church, He was not speaking of " the outward

[1] Revelation xviii. 4; *cf.* Jeremiah li. 6.

frame," as Alford calls it—the professing Church on earth, entrusted to human administration. The apostasy of *that* Church is clearly foretold in Scripture. "I know not"—says Canon Bernard in the *Bampton Lectures*, 1864—"I know not how any man, in closing the Epistles, could expect to find the subsequent history of the Church essentially different from what it is." But the Lord was speaking of the Church of which *He* is the builder, "the Church which is His Body, the fulness of Him that filleth all in all." That Church, we know, can never fail; His care for it can never cease, and His provision for its perfecting is assured.[1]

More than this, we have His promise, "Where two or three are gathered together in My Name, there am I in the midst of them." And the fact that this promise was given before the beginning of this Christian dispensation, is a further pledge that it will stand until the end. By its very terms, moreover, it is, as Dean Alford remarks, "independent of particular forms of government or ceremonies, and establishes a canon against pseudo-catholicism in all its forms." Wherever

_____
[1] Ephesians iv. 11-13.

two or three are gathered together in **His Name,** *there His presence is assured.*

Having regard to the incalculable importance of the subject, no apology is needed for this digression. Of the many who go over to Rome, and of the multitudes who are seeking to undo the work of the Reformation in England, there is not one who is not the dupe of false views about "the Church." And in other ways, and in wholly different spheres, Christians are misled or troubled by ignorance or error upon this subject.

Do not such false beliefs lead many to "bite and devour" their fellow-Christians because of denominational differences, or to accept the ministry of false teachers, and even of unconverted men, because this Church or that accredits them? "Judge not, that ye be not judged," someone will exclaim. But the very chapter which opens with these words [1] contains the warning, "Beware of false prophets"; and upon us it casts the responsibility of detecting them. The precept against judging relates to *motives*; the injunction to judge refers to the life and teaching of men who claim to be His ministers.

---

[1] Matthew vii.

To combat these false beliefs is strictly germane to the purpose of these papers. "Salvation is of the Jews," the Lord declared at the time when the apostasy of the nation was near its climax. For theirs were "the adoption, and the glory, and the covenants, and the giving of the law, and the service of God, and the promises." But not even in the days of its pristine purity and power did the Christian Church hold a position analogous to that of Israel under the former dispensation. For the Israelites, as such, enjoyed a vantage-ground of favour, in virtue of the Covenant. But in this dispensation the Church and its ordinances can do absolutely nothing to raise unregenerate men above the common level of sin and guilt and doom. Whether within the Church or outside the pale, they are "aliens from the commonwealth and strangers to the covenants." Salvation is only and altogether in and through the Lord Jesus Christ.

"Salvation is of the Jews," was true in the former dispensation. "Salvation is of the Church" was never true; and any Church which makes such a claim is anti-Christian.

With Cyprian, who championed the error, its falseness was modified by the fact that he meant the universal Church.   But men soon forget " that there is a deeper unity than that of external form. For the true communion of Christian men—the communion of saints upon which all Churches are built—is not the common performance of external acts, but the communion of soul with soul, and of the soul with Christ. . . . Subtler, deeper, Diviner, than anything of which external things can be either the symbol or the bond, is that inner reality and essence of union—'the unity of the Spirit.' " [1]

[1] Hatch's *Bampton Lectures*, 1880.

Doctrine of the Gospel

"Sanctify in your hearts Christ as Lord: being ready always to give answer *(apologia)* to every man that asketh you a reason concerning the hope that is in you, yet with meekness and fear."

1 Peter 3:15, R.V..

9

DOCTRINE OF THE GOSPEL

"IF Christ bore the punishment of my sins, how can I be punished for them?"

"And if He has not borne the punishment of my sins, how can I escape?"

"And in either case, how can my belief affect the fact? Either He bore my punishment, or He did not: if He did, my salvation is assured; and if He did not, my salvation is impossible."

When difficulties of this kind are raised by objectors or scoffers, they are best met by silence or rebuke. But when they are used to stumble ignorant but earnest inquirers after truth, it is but right that we should deal with them.

In common with many kindred difficulties, they spring from the prevailing habit of stating truth in language that has no express warrant in Scripture. And this habit is fostered by a popular misconception of the true character of faith.

In his "Historic Faith," Bishop Westcott marks

the distinction between faith and both credulity and superstition, and then goes on to enforce the still more needed warning that *conviction* is not faith. When the Gospel is so stated that knowledge of salvation becomes the obvious conclusion of a syllogism, the sinner may "find peace" without ever being "brought to God" at all. Divine truth can never clash with reason, but it may be entirely opposed to experience, and, seemingly, even to fact.

It was so in Abraham's case. He had nothing to rest upon but the bare Word of God, unconfirmed by anything to which he could make appeal. The Revisers' reading of Romans iv. 19 presents this with striking definiteness and force: "He considered his own body now as good as dead, and the deadness of Sarah's womb." But, looking to the promise of God, he did not waver. Abraham *believed God*, and it was counted to him for righteousness. And Abraham is "the father of all them that believe."

Distrust of God was the cause of the creature's fall; how fitting it is, then, that faith in God should be the turning-point of his repentance! It is this very element indeed that makes the

Gospel "the power of God unto salvation to everyone that believeth." With nothing to look back to but sin, and nothing to look forward to but wrath, the sinner, with facts and feelings and experience and logic all against him, accepts God's Word of pardon and peace. And he receives the blessing, not because he has mastered a syllogism, but because, like Abraham, he believes God. And he becomes a changed man, not because he has learned the shibboleths of a right creed, but because, by the truth of God, received in the power of the Spirit of God, he has been made "partaker of the Divine nature." He has been "born again, by the Word of God which liveth and abideth for ever."

But someone will say: "This does not answer the question—Was Christ punished for my sins, or was He not?" No, but it explains what ought to be our attitude toward every problem of the kind. It may be doubted, moreover, whether anyone could intelligently explain the question.

What do we mean by "punishment"? That we suffer for the sins of others, is one of the commonest experiences of life on earth. But this in no way lessens the burden of the guilty. Such suffering, moreover, is but a part of God's moral government of the world, whereas " punishment "—if we are to use words accurately and in a judicial sense—awaits the decrees of the great day. Does not the question confound punishment with judgment? A sentence of death, for example, is not the *punishment* for murder. It merely fixes the guilt and decrees the penalty.

First of all, let us take note of the fact that when we say that Christ bore the punishment of our sins, we are using language that is not found in Scripture. But someone will say : " Though it may not be expressed, it is implied, as, for example, in Isaiah liii." Here we may learn a lesson from a recent incident in the French Chamber. The War Office issued an order to the troops. A certain officer communicated it to his command in his own words. The Minister of War was attacked in Parliament for punishing him, and he gave this striking answer : " He committed an offence, and I removed him ; he paraphrased an order which it was his duty only to read."

What a lesson for the preacher of the Gospel !

Some truths there are which we can make our own; and these we can distribute, so to speak, in our own coinage. But when we have to do with spiritual truths of a transcendental character, it behoves us to keep to the very words in which they are revealed.

Do we not use wholly undue freedom, bordering too often upon flippancy, in presenting " the glorious Gospel of the blessed God "? The true minister will never forget that he is a savour either of life unto life or of death unto death, in all those to whom he proclaims it.

Isaiah liii. is the utterance of the covenant people in the day of their repentance. The figurative language of the sixth verse is derived from the sin-offering; that of the fifth is borrowed from the prison-house. And to interpret either aright, we must have recourse to the typology of the Old Testament and the teaching of the New.

In the sin-offering of the great day of atonement, the sins of the people were laid upon the scapegoat, at the door of the tabernacle of the congregation; and then the victim, bearing those sins, was led away to the solitary land. And so in 1 Peter ii. 24, 25 (which quotes Isaiah liii.), we read: "Who, His own self bare our sins in His own body to the tree." Bishop Ellicott's commentary suggests that the colloquial expression, "on-to" the tree—that is, up to the tree and upon it—would still better express the idiom of the original. But if theological reasons did not intervene, it would not be rendered "*on* the tree"; and if we have faith in the accuracy of Scripture, we shall fearlessly accept the inspired words.

What light then will the narrative of the Gospels throw on them?

That the night of the betrayal was a tremendous crisis that narrative affirms. "Save Me from *this hour*," was the prayer of the agony in the Garden. And when the Lord was surrounded by the priests and soldiers, He exclaimed: "This is *your hour and the power of darkness.*" Till then no hand had ever been laid upon Him, save in loving service; but now He was "delivered up." The Divine power which till then had shielded Him, now left Him to the hate and violence of men.

It may be urged that this was a necessary step to the cross. Such no doubt it was; but was it only this? The shadow of the cross had darkened all His path. But now a cloud unknown before was about to cover Him. No reverent spirit will attempt to lift the veil which hides the unrevealed mysteries of Gethsemane and Calvary. For "the secret things belong unto the Lord our God. But those things which are revealed belong to us, and to our children"; and can we not learn the meaning of the record from the types and prophecies of the Old Testament, and the doctrinal teaching of the Epistles? Men have faced martyrdom in its most dreadful forms without flinching; and He was the pattern Man. "He endured the cross, *despising* the shame." But that which crushed Him, that from which His whole being shrank with an intensity of horror and dread that we can never understand, was it not the imputation of sin?

We are in the habit of assuming that His work as the Sin-bearer began when He was nailed to the cross. But that was the act of the Roman soldiers, whereas *this* depended on the decree of God. And this was the death He dreaded—not the yielding up of His spirit, for death in that sense was the close of His sufferings,

the gate through which He passed to victory.
The cup which the Father had given Him to
drink was death in its primary and deepest sense,
as separation from God. Scripture speaks of it
as His " being made a curse for us." The meaning of such words is one of the mysteries of
our redemption. And yet, with extraordinary
levity and daring, we presume to enter this
" holiest of all."

In infinite grace, God has used the imagery of
the prison-house to give us as it were a glimpse
behind the veil. But instead of falling on our
faces in adoring worship, we sit down forthwith
to translate the bruises which came of our iniquities, and the stripes which bring us healing,
into the language of the police-court or the count-
ing-house.

That there are great realities behind these
words we know, for the figurative language of
Scripture is never exaggerated or fanciful. And
in respect of all that it concerns us to know, we
have Divine certainty. It was not that the guiltless died, as guiltless, for the guilty, for that
would be an outrage upon justice both human
and Divine ; but that " He who knew no sin

was made sin for us." And sin being thus imputed to Him, He expiated it by His death.

If the inquiry be pressed: "How could sin be so imputed to the sinless as to make a vicarious death efficient, or even justifiable?" no answer may be attempted. As Bishop Butler says: "All conjectures about it must be uncertain." "Nor," he adds, "has he any reason to complain from want of further information, unless he can show his claim to it." If anyone can solve the mystery of the imputation of sin to Christ, he will be able perchance to solve the further mystery of God's imputing righteousness to the sinner. And when he has achieved this, his faith will stand in the wisdom of men and not in the power of God. God retreats upon His own sovereignty and the believing sinner is satisfied with the Divine "It is written." Reason bows before the God of reason, and the reasoner becomes a disciple and a worshipper.

The Revised Version reading of the fifteenth chapter of first Corinthians warrants our laying strong emphasis on what I am contending for. The inspired Apostle thinks it necessary to remind the Corinthians of the Gospel he had preached to them, the Gospel by which they had been saved. "I make known unto you," he says, "*in what words* I preached it unto you." [1] And he adds that he had delivered to them what he had himself received of the Lord—the same solemn formula that he uses of the Lord's Supper.[2] And here are "the words": "That Christ died for our sins, according to the Scriptures; and that He was buried; and that He rose again the third day, according to the Scriptures."

The public facts of the death of Christ would in themselves be no Gospel for a sinner. Indeed, they might well give rise to "a fearful looking-for of judgment." What makes the record of that death a "Gospel" is that He died *for our sins, according to the Scriptures*. And here we pass into a sphere where human testimony is not only inadequate but impossible; the sinner is shut up to accept, or to reject, the Word of

---

[1] The fact that these words are a parenthesis immensely increases their force. The passage should read: "Now I make known unto you, brethren, the Gospel which I preached unto you, which also ye received, wherein also ye stand, by which also ye are saved—I make known, I say, in what words I preached it unto you—if ye hold it fast, except ye believed in vain." This last clause is explained by verse 14.

[2] 1 Corinthians xi. 23.

God. And this it is, I again repeat, which makes the Gospel "the power of God unto salvation."

The Gospel is not a veiled or conditional promise, but a public proclamation to be "preached to every creature." For "God was in Christ reconciling the world unto Himself"; and now grace is reigning. Christ "gave Himself a ransom for all." "He has put away sin by the sacrifice of Himself"; put away sin in such sense that God can now proclaim forgiveness to all, without distinction or reserve. And all that believe are justified. For, in virtue of the cross, God can now be "just, and the Justifier of him that believeth in Jesus."

And if we are asked to translate this marvellous revelation of Divine grace into the language of criminology or commerce, and to say whether Christ has paid the sinner's debt, or borne his punishment, the answer that becomes us is a refusal "to paraphrase the order." [1]

As I have already noticed, moreover, the Gospel

---

[1] One of the most startling and deplorable examples of this error that I have ever read will be found in Mr. W. T. Stead's pamphlet, "The Revival in the West." See especially page 7.

to the unsaved is never stated in the New Testament in the language of the sin-offering.[1] On believing, the sinner is brought within the Covenant. Then, and not till then, he becomes so identified with Christ in that death on Calvary that it is reckoned as his own. Hence the added words: "That we, *being dead to sins*, should live unto righteousness; by Whose stripes ye were healed."[2]

When the preacher's theme is "righteousness, temperance, and judgment"—when he seeks to probe the conscience and stir the heart; when he appeals to men's better nature, and warns them of the consequences of their sins—he is master of his subject, and can choose his words. But when, as the ambassador of Christ, he comes to proclaim the message of the Gospel, let him speak with solemn reserve, and let him (unlike "the many") refrain from "corrupting the Word of God."[3]

A closing word respecting this caution about the language of the sin-offering. I deprecate the thought that we should be limited or hindered in using Holy Scripture. Only let us beware of

---

[1] See pp. 50, 51, *ante*.

[2] 1 Peter ii. 24.

[3] 2 Corinthians ii. 17 (R.V.). The word for "corrupt," is formed from a word which signifies "huckster."

" huckstering " it in phraseology of our own. As I crossed Hyde Park on my way to Whitehall one morning, some years ago, I was startled by a pistol shot near by. As I turned I saw a man roll off one of the seats upon the ground. The poor wretch had shot himself. I ran across the grass to where he lay, and plied him with questions. He was past speech, but I saw by his look that he was conscious and understood my words. His life was ebbing, and if a message was to reach him it must be brief and quickly spoken. And as, in that solemn moment, I lifted my heart for guidance, the words that came to my lips were these, and I repeated them to the dying man :

" Surely He hath borne our griefs, and carried our sorrows : yet we did esteem Him stricken, smitten of God, and afflicted. But He was wounded for our transgressions, He was bruised for our iniquities : the chastisement of our peace was upon Him ; and with His stripes we are healed. All we, like sheep, have gone astray ; we have turned every one to his own way ; and the Lord hath laid on Him the iniquity of us all."

Were it not for the grace which condones the ignorance and error which mark our presentation of Divine truth, the ministry of the Gospel would be practically in abeyance. But let no man trade upon grace, and refuse to bring his thoughts and words to the test of Scripture. And above all, let everyone who claims to be a minister of the Gospel shun what savours of flippancy or levity in a sphere so solemn. Many a man who at heart is reverent and true falls into habits of speech about our Divine Lord, and the Gospel of His grace, which belie and dishonour his ministry. Let us seek to be imitators of him who, looking back upon a matchless life of service, in which he had received revelations beyond any entrusted to other men, wrote the words, " Unto me, who am less than the least of all saints, is this grace given, that I should preach among the Gentiles the unsearchable riches of Christ." [1]

---

[1] Ephesians iii. 8

Sonship and the New Birth

"Being born again...by the word of God, which liveth and abideth for ever."

1 Peter 1:23.

"As many as are led by the Spirit of God, they are the sons of God."

Romans 8:14.

10

SONSHIP AND THE NEW BIRTH

" A DAM was the son of God; all men, therefore, must be sons of God."

How eager men are to claim this relationship,
while utterly indifferent to the responsibilities and
duties which it involves! But it is a flagrant
fallacy to argue that because unfallen Adam was
the son of God, the descendants of fallen Adam
are also sons. And Scripture knows no such
sonship.

Of the Lord Jesus Christ it is written : " He
came unto His own, and His own received Him
not. But as many as received Him, to them
gave He the right to become the sons of God,
even to them that believe on His name : which
were born, not of blood, nor of the will of the
flesh, nor of the will of man, but of God." [1]

True it is that, when preaching to Athenian
idolaters, the Apostle Paul adopted the words of a

---

[1] John i. 11-13.

heathen poet : " For we are also His offspring." [1]
But no doctrine of sonship can be founded upon
this. The word here used is one of wide significance ; and the argument he based on it would
be equally valid if the lower creation were in-
cluded in it. The language of Hebrews ii. 14
also is perverted to support this figment. But,
as the sequel shows, " the children " there spoken
of are the " seed of Abraham." [2] Most certain it
is that all men are God's creatures. But they
only are children of God who have been begotten
of God ; and there is only one way in which
sinners can be thus begotten.

This truth has always been resisted by the
professing Church. The profane heresy of " the
brotherhood of Jesus," so popular to-day, is but
a phase of the old heresy of redemption by the
Incarnation, which, under the influence of pagan
philosophy, leavened the teaching of some of the
greatest of the Fathers. Not that they were so
heretical as their modern disciples and imitators.

---

[1] Acts xvii. 28.

[2] " For verily not of angels doth He take hold, but He taketh
hold of the seed of Abraham " (verse 16, R.V.). " We must not
here understand *mankind* as some have done " (ALFORD).

For while with them Calvary was indeed over-shadowed by Bethlehem, it was not reduced to being merely a display of heroic self-sacrifice. They did not deny the Atonement.

And the Western Church, though refusing saintship to those who thus erred, took refuge in a heresy more evil still. The great Augustine of Hippo was its most distinguished exponent. While rejecting the Alexandrian conception of a God "immanent" in human nature, he and his school were no less corrupted by Greek philo-sophy. The Deity of their theology was an alienated and angry God, between Whom and men depraved and doomed, the Church was a mediator. For "the bosom of the Church" afforded the only refuge from Divine wrath; and to bring men within that shelter was their aim.[1]

To this end, the simple baptism of the New Testament—a public confession of Christ by those whom the Gospel had won—was remodelled on pagan lines as a mystical regeneration and cleansing from sin, bringing the sinner into a

---

[1] "Augustine substituted an organized Church and a supernatural hierarchy for an ever-present Christ" (DEAN FARRAR).

sphere where a mystically-endowed priesthood could minister to him further grace.

But some one will exclaim : " Why speak of these heresies ? Positive truth is what is wanted." Yes, in these days people are intolerant of all denunciations of error. But the seeming triumph of Satan, from the day of the Eden Fall to the present hour, has been largely due to his skill in using " positive truth." Men would be startled by a direct denial of Divine truth ; so he adopts the very words in which it is revealed, and then corrupts them, or explains them away. Take, for example, the Lord's explicit declaration : " Ye must be born again." He does not challenge this : it is the creed of Christendom. But what does it mean ? Baptismal regeneration ! And the other " sacrament " will satisfy the Master's words about eating His flesh and drinking His blood. Thus the Word of God, while formally accepted, is made of none effect by the traditions of men.

It cannot be asserted too plainly that no one is a child of God who has not been born of God ; and that no sacrament, no ordinance of religion, can procure the new birth in any sense, or in any degree. The salvation of a sinner is God's work altogether. Baptismal regeneration was a doctrine of ancient paganism, but it has no place in Christianity. Scripture knows nothing of it. Never even once in the New Testament is water baptism mentioned in connection with the new birth, or with the Spirit's work. This is not an expression of opinion, but a statement of fact which anyone can test with the aid of a concordance.

That baptism is *referred to* in "the Nicodemus sermon" is, no doubt, the traditional view of the third chapter of John. But the judgment of a weighty minority of theologians, from Calvin to the late Bishop Ryle of Liverpool, bars the assertion that this is the "orthodox" interpretation of the passage. Dr. Ryle's "six reasons" for rejecting it seem to me indeed to make an end of controversy upon the subject.[1] The traditional view is practically vetoed by the glaring anachronism it involves. For the Lord reproved Nicodemus for his ignorance of a birth by water and Spirit. But how could he have known anything of Christian baptism? It had not yet been

---

[1] "Expository Thoughts on the Gospels."

instituted, and even the Apostles themselves knew nothing of it.

To fall back upon John's baptism only makes matters worse. For what relation had John's baptism to the new birth? But, we are told, the Jewish baptism of proselytes was a baptism of regeneration. Are we then to hold that the Lord's teaching about the Kingdom was based on a mere human ordinance, which had no Scriptural warrant, and which the Jews in days of apostasy derived from ancient paganism? The suggestion is positively profane.

We stand upon certainty when we aver, first, that the truth to which the Lord appealed was truth Divinely revealed, and that therefore it is in the Scriptures of the Old Testament that we must seek for the meaning of His words; and, secondly, that His words must imply redemption by blood, for on no other ground can anyone enter the Kingdom. In the sequel, recorded in verses 14–18, the Lord is not unfolding an alternative way of obtaining life; the birth by water and Spirit must, like the serpent lifted up, point to Calvary.

And, lastly, the water of John iii. 5 must have the same significance as the water of 1 John v. 6, 8—"This is He that came by water and blood, even Jesus Christ; not with the water only, but with the water and with the blood" (R.V.). And let us not forget the words which follow : "There are three who bear witness—the Spirit, and the water, and the blood." What then does the water signify? No one whose mind is not steeped in sacramentalism can imagine that in the three-fold "witness of God," baptism is here sandwiched between the Holy Spirit and the blood of Christ. And the attempt to explain the words by the fact recorded in John xix. 34 savours of a materialism that is wholly foreign to Christianity.

Such an explanation, moreover, is utterly in-adequate. The force of the language is that the mission and ministry of Christ were characterised by water and blood. It was not that at the death of Christ blood and water flowed from His pierced side; but that His coming, regarded as a whole, was "with the water and with the blood." This, which is plain even in our English version, is made very emphatic in the original by the change of the preposition in the sixth verse.[1]

But what is the significance of this ? The statement that the advent of Christ was characterised by blood is to be explained, not by the shambles, but by the types. It shuts out the "brotherhood of Jesus" lie, that He took flesh and blood in order to raise humanity by the splendid example of a perfect life and a martyr's death. It tells us that redemption was the great purpose of His coming. And this implies a ruin that allowed of no other remedy. Hence the emphasis with which it is asserted; hence, also, the hostility which it provokes in the human heart. The answer of the Jews was to crucify Him, thus aiding unwittingly in the fulfilment of His mission. His rejection by the Christianised Sadducees of to-day is as definite though not as brutal.

The Christian understands "the blood" by reference to the Hebrew Scriptures, which spell out for him the great truth of redemption. His

---

[1] The English reader can judge of the force of this preposition by its use in 1 Corinthians iv. 21, where the Apostle asks, "Shall I come unto you *with* a rod, or *in* love?" that is, "Is my coming to be characterised by severity or by love?" ("With" and "in" represent the same preposition in the Greek.)

thoughts turn back to the Passover, and with humble joy his faith finds utterance in the words, "Redeemed by the precious blood of Christ, as of a lamb without blemish and without spot." But so profound is the prevailing ignorance of the types that we fail to understand "the water."

As we have seen in preceding chapters, a redeemed sinner needs cleansing as really as a lost sinner needs redemption. And the sin-offering and the water of purification were for a redeemed people. And they cannot be separated; for it was to the sin-offering that the water of purification owed its ceremonial efficacy. It was because it had flowed over the ashes of the sacrifice that it availed to cleanse.

The sin-offering of Numbers xix. was as necessary to the Israelite as was the Passover. And Christ is the fulfilment of *all* the types. To the contemporaries of the Apostle, moreover, who, unlike ourselves, were well versed in Scripture, the meaning of all this was both clear and profound. For them such a phrase as that He "came with the water" needed no explanation. And, as Ezekiel xxxvi. tells us, when Christ returns in blessing to Israel His coming will be

"with the water only." But this is because His
first coming was "not with the water only, but
with the water and with the blood." Redemption is already accomplished.

That rite and that prophecy filled a large
and prominent place in Jewish theology and
Jewish hopes; and for a Rabbi to be ignorant
of them was as extraordinary and as inexcusable
as it would be for a Christian minister to be
ignorant of "the Nicodemus sermon." Hence our
Lord's indignant remonstrance : " Art thou the
teacher of Israel, and knowest not these things ? "

The wording of our Authorized Version, " Except a man be born of water *and of* the Spirit,"
lends support to the error of supposing the new
birth to be twofold. But the birth " of water
and Spirit " is so essentially one that in the next
verse, and again in verse 8, the Lord omits the
water, and in speaking of the same birth describes
it simply as " of the Spirit." [1]

---

[1] Many letters have reached me on this subject. Some still insist
that the birth by water is baptism—John's baptism, some say ; and
some even maintain that it is *natural* birth ! But birth by water is a
figment of Paganism. Scripture knows nothing of it. If such errors
had not a terrible spiritual power behind them, Dr. Hatch's *Hibbert
Lectures* would have killed this delusion. My own work, *The Buddha
of Christendom*, gives a summary of his statements. And see chapter
xii., *post*.

The time when the prophecy of Ezekiel xxxvi. and xxxvii. shall be fulfilled is called by the Lord Himself "the regeneration." [1] The only other passage where that word occurs is Titus iii. 5: "He saved us, by the washing of regeneration, and renewing of the Holy Ghost." The word here rendered "washing" is *loutron*. It is a noun substantive, not a verb. To render it "laver" would suggest a false exegesis, for a different, though kindred, word is used for "laver" in the Greek Bible. But it is a significant fact that in the only passage in that version where it is used in relation to sacred things it refers to the "water of purification." [2]

"The *loutron* of regeneration" therefore does not speak to us of the river or the font, but of the great sin-offering.[3] And this gives us a clue to its meaning in the only other passage where it occurs in the New Testament. I refer to Ephesians v. 26, where we read that Christ gave Himself for the Church "that He might sanctify

---

[1] Matthew xix. 28.

[2] "He that is baptized after touching a dead body, if he touch it again, what avails his *loutron*" (Ecclesiasticus xxxiv. 25).

[3] The sin-offering of Numbers xix.

and cleanse it with the *loutron* of water by the word."

By *the word*, mark. As we have seen, "the water of purification" owes its efficacy to the sin-offering. It is not to sacraments or human ordinances of religion that the Christian owes his cleansing, but to Calvary. In the type the Israelite obtained the benefits of the sacrifice by means of the water, and it is by "the word" that the believing sinner obtains the blessings of Calvary. Hence the language of the Epistle, "the *loutron* of water in the word."

The water of purification was, as we have seen, the water of regeneration; and it is by "the word" that the sinner is born again to God. The new birth has nothing to do with mystic acts or shibboleths after the pattern of ancient paganism. As Scripture declares, "we are born again by the word of God"—"the living and eternally abiding word of God." And to bar all error or mistake, it is added: "And this is the word which by the Gospel is preached unto you"—preached, as the Apostle has already said, "with the Holy Ghost sent down from heaven."[1] Not the Spirit without the word, nor the word without the Spirit, but the word preached in the power of the Spirit.

Men can fix time and place for ordinances, for ordinances relate to earth; but the new birth is from above. As the Lord said to Nicodemus—referring to the Ezekiel prophecy—"The Spirit breathes where He wills."[2] In Ezekiel xxxvi. we have the promise: "I will sprinkle clean water upon you, and ye shall be clean"—water, that is, which owes its cleansing efficacy to the sin-offering. And then, "I will put My Spirit within you."

The vision of the dry bones follows. You ask, How can sinners, helpless, hopeless, dead—as dead as dry bones scattered upon the earth—be born again to God? "Can these bones live?" is the question of Ezekiel xxxvii. And the answer comes: "Prophesy unto these bones, and say unto them, O ye dry bones, hear the word of the

---

[1] 1 Peter i. 12, 23, 25. In verse 25 (as in Ephesians v. 26) the word is *rēma*, and in verse 23 it is *logos*; but this does not affect the question here at issue.

[2] John iii. 8. *Pneuma* occurs some 370 times in the New Testament, and twenty-three times in John, but nowhere else is it rendered "wind."

Lord." Preach to dead, lost sinners; call upon them to hear the word of the Lord. This is man's part. Or if there be anything more, it is, " Prophesy unto the Breath: pray that the Spirit may breathe upon these slain that they may live." The rest is God's work altogether, for " the Spirit breathes where He wills." Not that there is anything arbitrary in His working. God is never arbitrary; but He is always Sovereign. Men preach; the Spirit breathes; and the dry bones live. Thus it is that sinners are born again to God.

Christendom and the Judgment

"The foundation of God standeth sure, having this seal, The Lord knoweth them that are His. And, Let every one that nameth the name of Christ depart from iniquity."

2 Timothy 2:19.

11

CHRISTENDOM AND THE JUDGMENT

MOST of the superstitions of Human religion may be traced ultimately to a Divine revelation. The pagan conception of atonement by blood, for example, could never have been evolved from the human mind. It comes from ancient Babylon; and Babylon was to the Old World what the apostasy of Christendom is to the New—the Satanic corruption of God's revelations to men.[1]

Though it has borrowed much from Babylon, the "Christian apostasy," being nearer to the truth than the pagan, is on that very account more dangerous. But there are two main characteristics, which mark off the true, in Christian doctrine and Christian life. Grace, as we have seen, has no counterfeit even in the so-called "Christian

---

[1] The infidel avers that the Christian doctrine of atonement by blood is derived from ancient paganism. But the pagan conception is obviously a corruption of the primeval revelation. For apart from its spiritual significance, as foreshadowing the work of Christ, the practice, if viewed apart from its spiritual meaning, is so absurd that it could never have originated save in a lunatic asylum!

religion." And another characteristic of Christianity is its distinctive hope.

The common belief that the errors of the Christian apostasy had their origin in the darkness of the Middle Ages is a mischievous delusion. They originated with the "orthodox" Fathers in the halcyon days of the "Primitive Church." The great Chrysostom—the most eminent of the early martyrs to the persecuting spirit of the "Catholics"—lamented that "all things which are Christ's in the truth—nay, even Christ Himself," were counterfeited in the heresies which even then prevailed. And, as the Christians' only safeguard, he urged "that they should betake themselves to nothing else but the Scriptures." What wonder then if in our own day the devout but uninstructed Protestant differs from an equally devout Romanist mainly in this, that he has a somewhat clearer view of the Cross of Christ. Both alike are in a position akin to that of men awaiting trial for a crime, but who are happy in expecting an acquittal. They are looking forward to death and judgment to decide their destiny.

But the believer in the Lord Jesus Christ

" cometh not into judgment, but hath passed out of death into life." [1] He has forgiveness of sins here and now. And he is not only forgiven, but justified. And he has peace with God ; and instead of looking forward to the day of wrath, he is called to " rejoice in hope of the glory of God." [2] With the religion of Christendom, the salvation of the soul is a prize to be won by saint-ship ; but the Scripture represents it as a blessing which grace bestows upon the sinner who believes. It is the starting-post and not the goal of the Christian's course.

Upon two main points which concern us here, the teaching of Christ is clear and explicit. The first is that, in the case of those to whom the Gospel comes, the consequences of accepting or rejecting Him are immediate and eternal. And, secondly, the final destiny of all will be decided prior to the resurrection. For the resurrection will be either " unto life," or " unto judgment." [3] And the redeemed will be raised in bodies like His own—" fashioned like unto His glorious body." This and not death, is the true hope of the Christian. Death is not the goal of life. It is rather

---

[1] John v. 24, R.V.   [2] Romans v. 1, 2.   [3] John v. 29, R.V.

a disaster and an outrage. And if faith can meet it without flinching, it is because God has "given us the victory through our Lord Jesus Christ."

These Gospel truths have been brought into fresh prominence in the Revival of the last half century. But it is to be feared that correlative truths which bear upon the Christian life have been somewhat overlooked. The Gospel of the religion of Christendom finds a fitting symbol in the crucifix. It leads its votaries to hope for the salvation of their souls through the merits of a dead Christ, and the mediation of the Church. But the Christian's faith rests upon the living Lord, in whom we are bidden to rejoice, receiving now "the end of our faith, even the salvation of our souls." But we must not forget that there is another salvation yet to come—"a salvation ready to be revealed in the last time." This is the "living hope" to which we have been "begotten by the resurrection of Christ from the dead."[1]

And we are thus brought into a new position, with new privileges and new responsibilities. The pardoned sinner can say with the Psalmist: "I sought the Lord, and He heard me, and

---

[1] 1 Peter i. 3, 5, 9.

delivered me from all my fears." But let him not forget the words which follow: "Come, ye children, hearken unto me: I will teach you the fear of the Lord." [1] If he has present and full deliverance from all *his* fears, it is that he may learn *the fear of the Lord.* We have been redeemed from the law "that we might receive the adoption of sons." [2] And to such the exhortation comes: "If ye call on Him as Father, who judgeth according to each man's work, pass the time of your sojourning here in fear;" not because redemption is in doubt, but because of the tremendous price which it has cost—"the precious blood of Christ." [3]

Though the redeemed shall never be arraigned before the dread tribunal of the great white throne, "every one of us shall give account of himself to God." [4] For "we must all be made manifest before the judgment-seat of Christ; that each one may receive the things done in the body, according to what he hath done, whether it be good or bad." And the Apostle adds: "Knowing, therefore, the fear of the Lord, we

---

[1] Psalm xxxiv. 4, 11.

[2] Galatians iv. 5.

[3] 1 Peter i. 17-19.

[4] Romans xiv. 12.

persuade men."[1] " Terror " is a sheer mistranslation. Fear of that kind, love casts out ; but, " knowing the fear of the Lord " is one of the characteristics of the child of God.

Just as in the hell of traditional theology all distinctions of responsibility and guilt are lost in the horrors of a common doom, so its heaven is but a fool's paradise, where the memories of earth will be so entirely effaced that all on which our personality depends will disappear. What wonder is it if men revolt against belief in such a hell, and the realities of the world to come are losing their influence upon the Christian life ? If the judgment-seat of Christ be not quite forgotten, it is regarded as a function resembling " speech day " at school, when industry and talent are rewarded, and the idle and disobedient are kept in the background, So much forgotten is it, indeed, that this simple statement of the plain teaching of Scripture will cause bewilderment and distress to many.

" But, will our *sins* be remembered?" some will ask. That no question of *guilt* can ever arise, we may be assured. In that sense the believer " shall

---

[1] 2 Corinthians v. 10, 11, R.V.

not come into judgment," and his sins shall be remembered no more. For him death and judgment have their counterpart in Christ's appearing as a sin-bearer, and His appearing again " without sin unto salvation." [1] No less definite, however, is the statement that in that day one " shall receive a reward," while another " shall suffer loss." [2] " Yes," someone will say, " but that relates to *service*." Precisely so. And this principle, perhaps, underlies the whole judgment of the redeemed. Only let us avoid the error which so soon corrupted the early Church, of separating off the " religious " from the " secular " element in Christian life. In all his relationships, and in the discharge of all his duties in life, the Christian is the servant of God, and as a servant he shall give account of himself to God.

" If this be true," I hear someone exclaiming, " I never can be happy again." The statement is deplorable. Unless the redeemed in glory are to sink to a lower level both morally and spiritually than that on which they stand on earth, happiness based on ignoring facts will be impossible. Moreover, the Divine purpose in redemption is the

---

[1] Hebrews ix. 27, 28. [2] 1 Corinthians iii. 14, 15.

glory of the Lord Jesus Christ; and the happiness of the redeemed cannot but be increased by everything which " manifests " what they are in themselves, and magnifies the grace of their salvation.

" The brotherhood-of-Jesus " cult has so corrupted us that we need to be reminded that our Saviour is the risen and glorified Lord, whose eyes are as a flame of fire, whose face is as the sun shineth in its strength, and out of whose mouth proceeds a sharp two-edged sword. A false peace may be attained by bringing Him down to our own level. But if, like " the beloved disciple," we have known what it means to see Him thus in His glory, and falling at His feet as dead, to hear Him say, " Fear not, . . . I am He that liveth, and was dead, and behold, I am alive for evermore, and have the keys of death and of hell," we have a peace which neither death nor hell can shake.[1]

The solemnity of being a Christian in a world that has rejected Christ, is growing deeper as the last apostasy develops. The Buddha of the popular religion of the day is the " brotherhood of Jesus " myth; and its devil is the obscene monster of ancient Babylonian paganism. But

[1] Revelation i. 12-18.

the Christian's Christ is "the Lord of glory," and his Satan is the god of this world — that awful being who "fashioneth himself into an angel of light." The "seducing spirits" of the last apostasy are not *unclean* spirits. They inculcate a more fastidious morality than Christianity itself will recognise; and under their influence Satan's ministers "fashion themselves as *ministers of righteousness*."[1]

The test of the true minister, therefore, is not zeal or piety, earnestness or purity of life; for under these evil spiritual guides, even "Christian Science" and "Spiritualism" excel in these respects. "Whosoever goeth onward [takes the lead, as a shepherd going before his sheep], and *abideth not in the teaching of Christ*, hath not God."[2] This is the only sure and vital test. And the same inspired Apostle demands: "Who is the liar but he that denieth that Jesus is the Christ?"[3]

That He is "THE CHRIST." It is not that He died, nor even that He died for our sins, for demon doctrine will accept this, and dwell upon

---

[1] 2 Corinthians xi. 14, 15, R.V.; 1 Timothy iv. 1-3.
[2] 2 John 9, R.V.   [3] 1 John ii. 22.

it with exquisite feeling. But that " He died
for our sins *according to the Scriptures* "; died
to make atonement for our sins ; died as the
fulfilment of the typical teaching of the Divine
religion of Judaism—the fulfilment of " all things
which were written in the law of Moses, and in
the Prophets, and in the Psalms, concerning
Him." This is " the doctrine of the Christ ";
and if a man has it not, then, no matter how
beautiful his teaching in other respects, no matter
how beautiful his character and life, the Holy
Spirit declares that " this is the anti-Christ, even
he that denieth the Father and the Son." And
let Christians who are trifling with these false
gospels, and recognising these false ministers,
bethink themselves that they shall have to give
account of themselves to God.

It is always sad when Christians fail to live
the Christian life, but the failure becomes dis-
astrous in presence of this latter-day development
of evil under the guise of good. For if the life
of those who have the doctrine of Christ com-
pares unfavourably with the life of men who
ignore or deny the doctrine, the doctrine itself
becomes discredited. But we must not lower the

standard of the Gospel. The remedy is not to veil the truth that God is love, but to proclaim anew the truth that God is light. Not to make less of the truth that Christ is Saviour, but to make more of the truth that He is Lord. We need to be ever reminded of the solemnities of Divine judgment, both in this "time of our sojourning," and at the judgment-seat of Christ.

"This man receiveth *sinners*" was the indignant protest of the Pharisees when the Lord called the fallen to His side. And if the Sadducees of our own day have different thoughts, it is not because they know more of grace, but because they have discovered, as they think, that there is no impassable gulf between sinful men and God. Theirs is the "gospel" which led to the Eden Fall—a "gospel" which attributes human qualities to God and latent divinity to man. And these prevailing currents of error have an influence on the thoughts and lives of Christians. "Revivalism," moreover, in some of its phases, leads in the same direction, though by another road. For though it has no real affinity with the "brotherhood-of-Jesus" cult, it encourages it, and seems allied to it. But if "the days are evil," let us give the greater heed to the Divine injunction, " Sanctify Christ in your hearts *as Lord*." And let the glory vision of the first chapter of the Revelation be kept more prominently in view. For Divine truth is the antidote to human error.

The Gospel brings peace to the sinner, not because it makes light of his sin, or lowers the inexorable claims of Divine perfection, but because it tells how Christ has made it possible for an absolutely righteous and thrice holy God to pardon and save absolutely sinful and evil men.

Hope of the Christian

"Blessed be the God and Father of our Lord Jesus Christ, who according to His great mercy begat us again unto a living hope by the resurrection of Jesus Christ from the dead."

1 Peter 1:3, R.V..

12

HOPE OF THE CHRISTIAN

THE figment of " baptismal regeneration " assumes that the new birth is peculiar to the Christian dispensation. But the striking fact that the new birth is never mentioned in the writings of the Apostle Paul, makes it plain that there is nothing distinctively Christian in the doctrine. No one who has not experienced the new birth can ever see the kingdom of God. This is a truth for all time, from the Eden Fall down to the judgment of the Great Day. But in this Christian dispensation it is merged in the higher truth of the baptism of the Holy Spirit, by which the sinner who believes becomes one with Christ.

And this truth of the oneness of the believer with Christ reminds us that the teaching of the types is in part by contrast. The sin-offerings of the law could neither take away sin, nor effect any change in the offerer. But " He was manifested to take away sins "; and the truth that Christ died for us has, for the believer, another side, namely, that " we died with Christ."[1] And let no one suppose that this is an experience to be attained by a life of special saintship. The chapter from which the words are quoted was addressed to those who knew so little of grace that they could raise the question, " Shall we continue in sin, that grace may abound ? "[2] It is not an experience, but a truth to be made the basis of an experience in a grace-taught life.

But there is yet another contrast here. Synonyms are few in Scripture, and the Cross means more than the *death* of Christ. Death was the Divine judgment upon the sin-bearer ; but " the Cross " speaks also of shame and the contempt of men, poured out without measure upon Him who died. And this is the separating power of Calvary. The Israelite returned from his sin-offering to his life in the camp. To the Christian, the exhortation comes, " Let us go forth therefore unto Him without the camp, bearing his reproach."[3] They who " mind

---

[1] Romans vi. 8, R.V. [2] Romans vi. 1.

[3] Hebrews xiii. 13. The original makes it clear that what is enjoined is not a great act of renunciation, but a continuing habit or attitude of soul

earthly things" are "the enemies of the Cross of Christ."[1]

But this is forgotten to-day. And the words that follow those last quoted remind us of a truth which is but little known. The pagan asceticism which corrupted the Church of the Fathers was due in part to the Gnostic error of regarding the body as an evil thing. And this error has so permeated the theology of Christendom that our translators misread the Apostle's words, "Who shall change the body of our humiliation?"[2] "The body of our humiliation"—this outward tabernacle of God-begotten men—is not "vile," but holy, and should be "yielded to God as an acceptable sacrifice."

Scripture distinguishes between the sin of Eve and the sin of Adam. Words that have been used unnumbered times in every age might be applied in a special sense to the Eden Fall: "The woman was weak, and the man was wicked." For, we are expressly told, "Adam was not deceived"—he sinned with his eyes wide open. But though the woman fell into transgression,

---

[1] Philippians iii. 18.
[2] Philippians iii. 21.

she was "thoroughly deceived."[1] The devil beguiled her into believing wrong was right, as he still beguiles so many of her children. What interval elapsed before Adam fell we know not. And it is idle to speculate what might have been had he stood true to God. But this we know, that sin meant not only death and judgment for man as a moral being under responsibility to God, but that it meant also his ruin as God's creature. And our bodies are involved in this creature ruin. And though they are within the ransom already paid, their redemption is still future.[2] Our bodies belong to the Lord Who died for us, and they are yet to be "fashioned like unto His glorious body."

Man may thus be regarded either as a doomed sinner, or as a ruined creature. He is not only Adam's son, but Eve's. And while death and judgment are past for the believer in Christ, and the salvation of the soul is a present blessing, yet, *as a creature*, the Christian still groans under the ruin. "Even we ourselves groan within

---

[1] 1 Timothy ii. 14. Even the Revised Version fails to notice the intensified form of the word as used of Eve.

[2] For redemption includes taking possession of what has been ransomed.

ourselves, waiting for our adoption, to wit, the redemption of our body."

This is "salvation by hope." But the hope is far removed from doubt. For God has promised, and the work is His. The redeemed sinner is "fore-ordained to be conformed to the image of His Son." [1]

" What, then, shall we say to these things? If God be for us, who can be against us? He that spared not His own Son, but delivered Him up for us all, how shall He not with Him also freely give us all things? Who shall lay anything to the charge of God's elect? It is God that justifieth. Who is He that condemneth? It is Christ that died, yea, rather, that is risen again, Who is even at the right hand of God, Who also maketh intercession for us. Who shall separate us from the love of Christ? Shall tribulation, or distress, or persecution, or famine, or nakedness, or peril, or sword? As it is written, For Thy sake we are killed all the day long; we are accounted as sheep for the slaughter. Nay, in all these things we are more than conquerors through Him that loved us. For I am persuaded, that neither death, nor life,

---

[1] See Romans viii. 20-29.

nor angels, nor principalities, nor powers, nor things present, nor things to come, nor height, nor depth, nor any other creature, shall be able to separate us from the love of God, which is in Christ Jesus our Lord." [1]

But this is by no means what men " say to these things." The inspired Apostle goes on to speak of great dispensational problems, mysteries of the Divine purposes for earth. He tells of the goodness and severity of God ; how Israel, the covenant people, has been set aside, and Gentiles, who have no covenant, have been called to the highest place of privilege and blessing. But Israel fell through unbelief, and the Gentile stands by faith. The Gentile, therefore, shall be " cut off," and Israel grafted into the olive tree again. The devil sometimes wins the skirmish ; God always wins the battle. And God's purposes, that have seemingly been thwarted by sin, shall at last appear as part of one great plan which includes the fulfilment of them all. And the contemplation of this leads the Apostle to fall upon his knees in adoring wonder, as he exclaims, " O the depth of the riches both of the wisdom and knowledge of God! how

---

[1] Romans viii. 31-39.

unsearchable are His judgments, and His ways past finding out!"[1]

But there are pulpits without number in this "Christian" land that know nothing of these great dispensational truths. And even men who are Bible students, and spiritual withal, blindly pervert them into a denial, or at least a weakening, of the great revelation of grace of which they are a part. How different the Divine purpose with which they have been given us, witness the words that follow:—"I beseech you therefore, brethren, by the mercies of God, to present your bodies a living sacrifice, holy, acceptable to God, which is your reasonable service."[2]

Your bodies, mark. He would thus stamp out the pagan heresy of the "vile body," which is so natural to us. For even "the body of our humiliation" is holy, and will prove an acceptable sacrifice. And the exhortation is not based upon terror or doubt, but upon "the mercies of God." For while Law thunders forth, "Thou shalt not," and points to the great white throne and the day of wrath, Grace speaks with the voice of entreaty, and appeals to "the mercies of God."

---

[1] Romans xi. 33   [2] Romans xii. 1.

And yet a warning is needed here. Grace is not a display of Divine weakness ; nor does it lead to levity in those whom it blesses. It is the crowning revelation of God's sovereignty, and it trains men for a life of self-control and righteousness and godliness. And, as we have seen, the record of each life is yet to be unfolded at the judgment-seat of Christ. The practical exhortations which follow the entreaty lead up to the solemn warning that " Each one of us shall give account of himself to God." [1] Our apprehension of the dignity and blessedness of the Christian life must not make us forget its solemnities.

But the redeemed are " fore-ordained to be conformed to the image of His Son, in order that HE might be the firstborn among many brethren." [2] The glory of Christ is the supreme purpose in our redemption. While this fact brings confidence and joy to the Christian, unbelief resents it. In all "humanity gospels" man is first, not God, and redemption is only a fitting act of reparation upon God's part for permitting sin to come into the world, or at best a

[1] Romans xiv. 12.
[2] Romans viii. 29.

sublime scheme for the elevation of the race.
Such is the teaching which is popular to-day.

Unlike these false evangels, the Calvinistic
gospel is, on its positive side, both true and
Scriptural. But though Calvin's apprehension
of truth was far in advance of modern "Calvin-
ism," it was narrowed by the theology of the
Latin fathers, and especially of Augustine, by
whom the great revelation of grace was never
grasped.[1] Universal redemption is utterly false;
but universal reconciliation is a Divine truth.
It is indeed an accomplished fact. And in virtue
of it, the (lower) creation shall yet be delivered
from the bondage of the corruption (to which
man's sin has subjected it) into the liberty of
the glory of the children of God. But the deliverance of the creature is still future. For
while the sinner receives the reconciliation when
he believes in Christ, "the earnest expectation
of the creation waiteth for the revealing of the
sons of God."[2]

And in contrast with the unintelligent groan of

---

[1] His *Confessions* give us the struggles of a true and earnest soul
toward light that he never reached.

[2] Romans viii. 19–21.

the creation, the groan of those "who have the firstfruits of the Spirit" is instinct with hope. And both the blind expectation of the creature and the intelligent yearning of spiritual men shall be satisfied in the day of "the manifestation of the sons of God." "Beloved, now are we the sons of God," a further word declares, "And it doth not yet appear what we shall be; but we know that when He shall appear, we shall be like Him; for we shall see Him as He is." [1]

"When He shall appear." Here the ways divide, and what passes for "the Christian religion" definitely parts company with Christian truth. That "He shall come to judge the quick and the dead" is, no doubt, an article in the creed of Christendom. But with most men even this is unreal. And how, moreover, can it be described as *a hope*? The Christian has been "begotten to a living hope." And this hope is no mere dogma, no vague forecast, no "cunningly devised fable." It moulds character and controls conduct. "He

---

[1] 1 John iii. 2. It cannot be an accident that the two apostles who were specially used to convey this truth to the Church of God are the two who alone were permitted to see Him in glory after the ascension (Acts ix.; Rev. i,).

that hath this hope set on Him purifies himself, even as He is pure." [1] The grace of God that
brings salvation teaches those whom it saves, and
its teaching leads them to live "soberly, righteously, and godly in this present world; looking
for the blessed hope and appearing of the glory of
our great God and Saviour Jesus Christ." [2]

"I will come again and receive you to Myself"
was His parting promise on the night of the betrayal. Does this point to the great day of wrath?
The suggestion is absurd. But, we are told, it
means the death of the believer. Here we may
sadly admit that such a belief is not more false
and foolish than many another that is popularly
held. Death is not His coming again to us, but
our going to Him. And while, for the Christian,
death has no terrors—for sin is gone, and therefore
it has lost its sting—it is none the less an outrage,
bringing home to us the fact of our still unrepaired
ruin as fallen creatures.

And while the "intermediate state" is one of
rest and blessedness, consciously enjoyed with
Christ, we must guard against the sentiment which
connects it with thoughts of glory and "the

[1] 1 John iii. 3.　　　[2] Titus ii. 11-13, R.V.

activities of higher service above." The condition
of the dead in Christ is as definitely one of ex-
pectancy as is that of the living Christian here.
There can be no glory and no service until the
realisation of the hope to which they were begotten by His resurrection from the dead.

For the dead in Christ, resurrection is the crown
and climax of redemption. The Lord Jesus Christ
has triumphed over death. But more than this,
He "gives the victory *to us*." Death therefore has
no longer any claim upon His people. It is one of
the "mysteries"[1] of the faith that, at the coming
of the Lord, His people then living on earth shall
pass at once to glory, "with death untasted and
the grave unknown." The corruptible shall *put on*
incorruption, the mortal immortality. And "*then*
shall be brought to pass the saying that is written,
Death is swallowed up in victory."[2]

Such, then, is the distinctive hope of Christianity : not pardon, not peace, most certainly not
death, but the appearing in glory of Him Whom
the world last saw as "the Crucified Jew," Whom

---

[1] A "mystery" is a once hidden but now revealed truth or purpose
of God.

[2] 1 Corinthians xv. 51-57 ; and see 1 Thessalonians iv. 15-17.

His people worship as enthroned at the right hand of God. For what constitutes a Christian is not accepting the Christian's creed, but accepting Christ as Saviour and Lord. It is a question of personal loyalty and love. When the Apostle Paul took up the pen to sign the Epistle to the Corinthians, he added the solemn postscript, "If any man love not the Lord Jesus Christ let him be accursed. The Lord is coming." And to those "who have loved His appearing" will be given "the crown of righteousness" in that day.

Although this is in the very warp and woof of the Christian revelation, it has, I repeat, no place in the creed of Christendom, and it is generally ignored in the teaching of the pulpit. For while the pulpit is much concerned with the Christian life and the ordinances of religion, it is strangely economical of truth that is the power of the Christian life, and to which ordinances owe their significance and value.

Even the Lord's Supper, designed to link the Coming with the Cross, is reduced to the level of the cult of the crucifix. With the majority of Christians it is nothing but a memorial of a dead Christ. It is most truly a showing forth the

Lord's death, but it is a showing forth His death *till He come.* It is not with a dead Christ that we have to do. Our Lord and Saviour is the Christ Who died, but Who rose again, and Who is alive for evermore. "Do this in remembrance of ME" is His word to all who mourn His absence and long for His return. "Surely I come quickly" are the last words that have reached earth from heaven; and "Even so, come Lord Jesus," is the response He looks for from His people.[1]

---

[1] Rev. xxii. 20.

The New Apostasy

"I am...the truth."

"Believest thou not that I am in the Father, and the Father in Me? the words that I speak unto you I speak not of Myself."

"The word which ye hear is not Mine, but the Father's which sent Me."

"Heaven and earth shall pass away, but My words shall not pass away."

Matthew 24:35.

13

THE NEW APOSTASY

THERE are two sources to which we can look for light as to the character and ways of God—Nature and Revelation. If God has spoken —if the Bible be what the Master declared it to be—the Divine light of Nature must pale before it, and we need no other guide. But if the new and seemingly popular estimate of the Bible be accepted, it is blindly stupid to appeal to that sort of book against the clear testimony of Nature.

And what will Nature tell us about God? Trumpet-tongued it will proclaim His goodness and His severity. "He that cometh to God must believe that He is, and that He is a rewarder of them that diligently seek Him." His existence Nature proclaims, and Revelation assumes. "The fool hath said in his heart, there is no God." In *his heart*, mark; he whispers it to himself in secret. The crass folly that would announce it

openly is not even contemplated. There is no
darkness like that which covers us when a strong
clear light is quenched. And the only atheists
are the apostates, men who have turned away
from Christianity.

But the teaching of Nature is that He is a
rewarder of *them that seek Him.* His goodness
is for those who merit it; for the rest there is
nothing but severity. As an infidel writer puts it,
"Nature knows no such foolery as forgiveness of
sins." Nature is stern, unpitying, remorseless in
punishing. And Nature is but another name
for God.

If any one disputes this, it is easily put to the
test. Outrage the laws of health, and you will
suffer to your dying day. Inflict a wound upon
your body, and you will carry the scar to your
grave. Seize the hot bar of the fire-grate, and
as you writhe in pain go down upon your knees
and with deepest penitence and agonized earnestness make your prayer to Nature's God.
Your prayer will bring you no relief. You have
sinned against Nature and you will seek forgiveness in vain, for Nature is relentless.

But you exclaim, "This is not *my* God." Are

there two Gods then? The God—by whose inexorable laws your burnt hand will cause you excruciating pain, and bear wound-marks while you live—is the same God who rained fire and brimstone upon the Cities of the Plain; Who gave up the old world to the destruction of the Flood; Who, because of a single sin, passed the awful death-sentence under which the teeming millions of earth still groan. There is but one God. The God of the Bible is the God of Nature.

"But," you say, "the Bible speaks of His infinite love and mercy, and His readiness to forgive." Yes, but Nature has no such voice; and I ask again, what is the Bible to which you appeal? Is it the Christianised sceptic's book of piety? or is it the Scriptures which the Lord Jesus described as "words proceeding out of the mouth of God"?

You will plead, perhaps, that it is upon the New Testament you rely, whereas this teaching of Christ related to the Hebrew Scriptures, and belonged to the ministry of His humiliation, when He had so "emptied Himself" that He spoke only as a man. But your allegation of fact is entirely contrary to fact. In His ministry after the resurrection, and on the eve of His ascension to the right hand of God, the Lord Jesus, speaking with full Divine knowledge, accredited the Hebrew Scriptures in the plainest and fullest way. The old *Kenosis* heresy, therefore, is of no avail whatever here.

The following is the record and description of His ministry *after He was raised from the dead*. Referring back to His teaching in the days of His humiliation, when, according to the critics, He spoke as a blind and ignorant Jew, He said to the disciples, "These are My words which I spake unto you, while I was yet with you, how that all things must needs be fulfilled, which are written in the law of Moses, and in the Prophets, and in the Psalms, concerning Me."[1]

And the record adds, "Then opened He their mind, that they might understand the Scriptures." The Epistles of the New Testament give proof that He taught them to accept and revere the Books of Moses as God-breathed Scripture; and, as the result of *their* teaching, every Christian Church for eighteen centuries thus accepted and

---

[1] Luke xxiv. 44.

revered them. But the Higher Critics tell us that His teaching was false, and that these beliefs of His disciples were a delusion.

Now mark what this involves. Evidence, whether of witnesses or of documents, is tested before we accept it. To require confirmation of every statement would, of course, be unreasonable. For if every statement could be proved independently, further evidence would be unnecessary. But we deal with such portions as admit of being tested, and if these prove unreliable we reject the whole as worthless. Yet the critics tell us that in the sphere in which alone the Lord's teaching admits of being thus tested, it is unreliable and false; and yet they call upon us to accept His teaching in the sphere of transcendental truth.

Take the case of the Pentateuch, for example. The Lord spoke of forgiveness and life for sinful men. But these blessings were declared to be dependent on His Person and work, as the antitype and fulfilment of "all that Moses in the Law and the Prophets did write." Therefore, to reject the scheme of redemption by blood, as unfolded in the Books of Moses, and yet to believe in redemption by Christ, is intellectually contemptible. And remember the Lord's teaching about the Books of Moses is opposed merely to the theories and assumptions of the critics; whereas, His teaching about forgiveness is opposed to the clear and emphatic testimony of Nature; and Nature is a synonym for God. For the great wonder—the mystery—of the Christian faith is not punishment, but pardon.

And yet this is the attitude of many an eminent scholar, and the testimony of many a popular pulpit, in these strange days of intellectual conceit and spiritual apostasy. If the "critical hypothesis" is wrong, the rejection of one important part of the Lord's teaching is sheer blasphemy; if it be right, the acceptance of the other part of His teaching is sheer credulity. For the test of credulity is not the truth or error of what is believed, but the grounds on which the belief is based. I repeat, therefore, that if the Lord was deceived in relation to matters within our competence to test, it is folly to accept His teaching in a higher sphere. Here, as in mechanics, nothing is stronger than its weakest part. Judged out of their own mouths, the "Higher Critics" are chargeable either with blasphemy or credulity.

Just as with the old apostasy of Christendom, so is it with the new; its most successful champions are men whose piety and zeal command respect. But the Christian who knows "the fear of the Lord," and who looks forward to the judgment-seat of Christ, will not be betrayed by Church ties or personal influence into acknowledging the ministry of any man who is on the side of either apostasy.

And in writing thus I am not unmindful of the difficulties which beset the student of Scripture; difficulties, some of which are as perplexing as those which mark the ways of God in nature. The question at issue, moreover, is not whether Moses wrote the Pentateuch in the sense in which Paul wrote the Epistle to the Romans, or whether earlier documents may not have been incorporated. These are questions within the legitimate scope of criticism; and I am neither an enemy of criticism nor a champion of traditional "orthodoxy."

But in spite of the continually accumulating mass of evidence in favour of their authenticity, "the Mosaic Books" are held to be literary forgeries of the Exilic era. In proof of this the German rationalists have put together evidence which is deemed full and clear, and their English disciples assume that therefore it must be true. But no one who has any experience of proceedings in our courts of justice—no " man of affairs," indeed—could be duped by a blunder so puerile as that of supposing that a case is necessarily true because evidence which is full and clear can be adduced in its support. The genuineness of the Pentateuch is clearly established by positive proofs which are incontestable ; and the " critical hypothesis " of its origin not only dislocates the whole framework of Scripture, but is utterly destroyed by the single fact that the Books of Moses constituted the Bible of the Samaritans.

This so-called " Higher Criticism," indeed, outrages every principle of true criticism. Most of its English exponents limit its operation to the Hebrew Scriptures, but Professor Cheyne's *Encyclopædia Biblica* gives proof of what Baur established half a century ago, that it is equally successful when applied to the New Testament. As for Hastings' *Bible Dictionary*, the organ of the Driver School, the book has not even the merit of consistency. For while in its contemptuous repudiation of the teaching of our Divine Lord it is as profane and evil as the *Encyclopædia*, the unwary are deluded by the *quasi*-Christian tone which pervades it. It is a stupid and impossible compromise between rationalism and faith.

The consistent rationalist is entitled to respect, for his position is intellectually unassailable. But those who accept the rationalist's estimate of the Bible and yet maintain its inspiration are deficient either in honesty, in courage, or in brains. " In the hands of Christian scholars," Professor Driver tells us, " criticism pre-supposes the inspiration of the Old Testament." But criticism is unprejudiced. It pre-supposes nothing. Men who have reached faith through scepticism counted the cost when entering the path of criticism. But men who pose as critics and yet pre-suppose the Divine authority of the Bible, are like fraudulent company promoters, who lead the public to believe their fortune is staked upon the venture, when, in fact, they are insured against the risks of it. Their attitude betokens the weakness of superstition, rather than the fearlessness of criticism.

One writer holds Oliver Cromwell to have been a saint, another holds him to have been a fraud; but what would be thought of a writer who maintained that he was *both*! And from an intellectual point of view, the position of the Hastings' *Dictionary* school of critics is equally impossible.

And it is not as though these men had the field to themselves. They have been refuted again and again by scholars as competent as themselves— Hebraists, archæologists, theologians. No one who has studied the Divine scheme of prophecy or the typology of Scripture, no one who is versed in the science of evidence, would accept the "critical hypothesis" of the Pentateuch. But, like the Jesuits, the critics never discuss, never reply. They ignore everything that is urged by their opponents; and, with the dull tenacity of fetich worshippers, they keep to reiterated appeals to "modern criticism." We can understand why Paul wrote of the critics of Apostolic days: "Professing themselves to be wise they became fools!"

But some who will read these pages will plead that they have not the opportunity, and possibly not even the capacity, to master this controversy. And to such I would address myself briefly in conclusion. In writing these pages I have used the Pentateuch as a text-book. And if the "critical hypothesis" be right, this is altogether ignorant and wrong. But in this I have followed the teaching of the Lord Jesus Christ, and the suggestion that He can have deceived and mis-led me is profane. For the allegation that it was only during His humiliation that He accred-ited the Books of Moses is, as we have seen, a sheer mis-statement. In none of His teaching, moreover, was He retailing "current Jewish notions"; but, as He declared again and again with extreme solemnity, He was uttering words which *God had given Him* to speak. And after the Resurrection He repeated and enforced the teaching of His earthly ministry, and sent out His disciples to proclaim it to the world.

Indeed, these *Kenosis* theories are merely the sophistry of German controversialists, adopted blindly by their English disciples, to conceal the mingled weakness and profanity of their scheme. This being so, I make nothing of such facts as that the "Higher Critics" are in a minority, and that no English theologians of the first rank have declared upon their side. For it may be that, in "the deepening gloom" of this infidel apostasy all "the wise and prudent" may yet fall to the side of error. The boast of the critics that all scholarship is with them is glaringly false; but let us suppose that it were true. I appeal to the humblest Christian who reads these pages to face the question fearlessly, with a mind steeped in the spirit of the words: "Let God be true, but every man a liar."

Every man. Suppose the whole apparatus of organized Christianity—every scholar and ecclesiastic and minister in Christendom—should yet be ranked on the side of the critics. What then? In darker days now past, the whole apparatus of organized Christianity was upon the side of the *religious* apostasy of Christendom. And in those evil days the children of truth were confronted by persecution full-fraught with all the terrors that religious hate could devise, whereas to us the word comes aptly, "Ye have not yet resisted unto blood."

What then shall be our attitude toward this new apostasy? Shall the nominal roll of its adherents decide the measure of our confidence in the Lord Jesus Christ as a Teacher?

We have reached a crisis where the ways divide. In many a congregation, and in every Church, the Christian needs to be reminded of the forgotten realities of the judgment-seat of Christ. Recalling the Master's words, " If ye believed Moses ye would also believe Me, *for he wrote of Me*," let him remember also the solemn warning, " Whosoever shall be ashamed of Me, and *of My words*, in this adulterous and sinful generation, of him also shall the Son of Man be ashamed when He cometh in the glory of His Father."

It is not as though the Lord's teaching on this subject were matter of controversy or of doubt. The " Higher Critics " admit without reserve that He believed that " Moses wrote of Him "; but they declare, as " an assured result of modern criticism," that in this the Lord was deceived and in error. Let the Christian then, as he shall give account at the judgment-seat, fearlessly, and without one lingering thought of unbelief, denounce this " assured result of criticism " as a profane falsehood. " Let God be true, but every man a liar."

If a gulf separates us from the Roman Catholic, it is not because we would " un-Christianise " him. Neither is it because there is error in his creed; for creeds are human, and all of them are marred by error. But it is because the distinctive errors of the Church of Rome directly touch the honour of the Lord Jesus Christ. And for precisely the same reason, a gulf as wide separates us from the " Higher Critic."

The critic and the Christian have not the same Christ. The Christ whom the Christian worships is He Who was God, and yet became Man; Who " counted it not a prize to be on an equality with God, but emptied Himself." So emptied Himself that He did not even claim a man's liberty, but subjected His own will to the will of God. Subjected it so unreservedly, that even the words He uttered were not His own, but the words of the Father Who sent Him. And to silence every possible plea for unbelief, we are Divinely told that " to Him the Spirit was given without measure."

But the mythical " Jesus " of the " Higher Critic " was one whose lips gave out Divine truth and human error in an undivided stream ;

one who was so entirely wanting in spiritual intelligence that he believed the error to be truth, and in words of solemn warning and command claimed acceptance of it as Divine.

In all the sad and evil history of the professing Church, no profaner heresy has ever arisen. It is practically a denial of " the Deity of Christ." It is absolutely anti-Christian.

Neither learning nor logic, therefore, is needed to make the true-hearted disciple turn from it with abhorrence. For it outrages all his spiritual instincts. To these instincts it is that, in view of kindred errors in the infant Church, the Apostle makes appeal: " These things," he says, " have I written unto you concerning them that would lead you astray. And as for you, the anointing which ye received of Him abideth in you, and *ye need not that any man teach you.*" Reason is always on the side of truth. But when the honour of the Lord is in question, spiritual instincts are a safer guide even than reason.

SCRIPTURE INDEX

SIR ROBERT ANDERSON LIBRARY SERIES

THE COMING PRINCE
This is the standard work on the marvelous prophecy of Daniel about the AntiChrist and the Seventy Weeks. It deals fully with the details of the chronology and with the vexing questions of the last of the Seventy Sevens.

FORGOTTEN TRUTHS
The author shares valuable insight into the difficulty for some people caused by the delay of our Lord's return, as well as other truths seemingly irreconcilable because of finite human minds.

THE GOSPEL AND ITS MINISTRY
A study of such basic Christian truths as Grace, Reconcilation, Justification and Sanctification. In the author's own direct, yet devotional, style these truths are stated, then emphasized; so that the skeptic becomes convinced and the believer is blessed.

THE LORD FROM HEAVEN
A devotional treatment of the doctrine of the Deity of Christ. This differs from other works in that it offers indirect testimony of the Scriptures as to the validity of this doctrine. This book is not written to settle doctrinal controversy, but rather it is a Bible study that will deepen the student's conviction, while giving a warm devotional approach.

Sir Robert Anderson Library

REDEMPTION TRUTHS
The author presents unique insights on the gift offer of salvation, the glory of Sonship and the grandeur of eternity's splendor.

THE SILENCE OF GOD
If God really cares, why has He let millions on earth suffer, starve and fall prey to the ravages of nature? Why has He been silent for nearly two millennia? The author gives a thorough and Scriptural answer. He also discusses the subject of miracles today with excellent answers. Here is a "must" for serious Bible students.

TYPES IN HEBREWS
A study of the types found in the book of Hebrews. Anderson ties the revelation of God to the Hebrew nation to the full revelation of the Church of Jesus Christ, with the premise that God's provision for the Jew was a forerunner of the blessings for the Christian. The author moves from type to type with his own pithy comments and then augments them with the comments of his nineteenth century contemporaries.